Becoming a Disciple Maker

21 DAYS TO
Becoming a Disciple Maker

JIM BRITTS

CHURCHLEADERS PRESS

21 Days to Becoming a Disciple Maker

Copyright © 2023 Outreach, Inc.

All rights reserved. No part of this publication may be reproduced, distributed, or transmitted in any form or by any means, without prior written permission.

Scripture quotations are taken from the Holy Bible, New International Version. Copyright © 1973, 1978, 1984, 2011 by Biblica, Inc.® Used by permission.
All rights reserved worldwide.

First Edition: Year 2023
21 Days to Becoming a Disciple Maker / Outreach, Inc.
Paperback ISBN: 978-1-958585-59-7
eBook ISBN: 978-1-958585-60-3

CHURCHLEADERS P R E S S

CONTENTS

INTRODUCTION 7	DAY 14 80
DAY 1 15	DAY 15 84
DAY 2 20	DAY 16 88
DAY 3 25	DAY 17 93
HABIT #1 30	**HABIT #4** 98
DAY 4 31	DAY 18 99
DAY 5 35	DAY 19 104
DAY 6 39	DAY 20 109
DAY 7 46	DAY 21 114
HABIT #2 50	**CLOSING WORDS** 118
DAY 8 51	APPENDIX A 121
DAY 9 55	APPENDIX B 122
DAY 10 60	APPENDIX C 124
DAY 11 65	APPENDIX D 128
	APPENDIX E 129
HABIT #3 71	
DAY 12 72	ABOUT THE AUTHOR AND
DAY 13 76	ACKNOWLEDGMENTS 133

INTRODUCTION

Before you go on this journey . . .

Imagine standing in a backyard pool with several friends and family surrounding you. You have the privilege of baptizing someone that you led into a relationship with Jesus and have been discipling. As you pull them back up from the water to an eruption of cheers, your heart pounds out of your chest with joy. You look at your newly baptized friend who is smiling from ear to ear and reach out for a celebration hug. How could it get any better than this?

But then, your friend's family joins you in the pool and you step to the side so that your friend can baptize each of them in turn. Your friend has been passing on the discipling learned from you, and now the whole family has all pursued a committed relationship with Jesus! And Jesus is transforming them. Addictions are being broken. Broken relationships are being restored. Bad habits are being replaced by holy living. And their friends and co-workers are starting to notice and desire these changes in their own lives. Several of these family members have started Bible study discipleship groups with their friends. The ripples from this one person you discipled are spreading and it is obvious God is moving.

What emotions would you be feeling watching this scene play out? Where would that scene fit in your list of highlights as a Jesus follower?

Do you realize that this scene is not just *possible* for you, but it is actually Jesus' *plan* for you many times over throughout your lifetime?

Unfortunately, there are very few Christians who have ever experienced a scene like this. Which is why I wrote this short book: for those who want to bring that scene to reality in their lives.

Who should read this?

> *A farmer went out to sow his seed. As he was scattering the seed, some fell along the path, and the birds came and ate it up. Some fell on rocky places, where it did not have much soil. It sprang up quickly, because the soil was shallow. But when the sun came up, the plants were scorched, and they withered because they had no root. Other seed fell among thorns, which grew up and choked the plants. Still other seed fell on good soil, where it produced a crop—a hundred, sixty or thirty times what was sown. Whoever has ears, let them hear.*

Matthew 13:3-9

I've sat one-on-one with hundreds of Christians over the past few decades and studied Jesus' parable of the four soils with them. On a napkin, I often write out these simple definitions of each soil:

Path = Not interested

INTRODUCTION

Rocky soil = Too Shallow

Thorny soil = Too Busy

Good soil = Fruitful

Then I ask two really simple questions:

1. Which of these four soils do you want to live your life on?

You already know what everybody answers because it's your answer, too. Of course, you want to be on the good soil. Who wouldn't?

2. In all honesty, which of these four soils does your life most closely resemble?

More than 90 percent of those I ask give the same (slightly ashamed) answer: Honestly, the words "too busy" are a much more accurate description of my life than the word "fruitful." And honestly, this would have been my answer for much of my life.

If it's yours, too, then great news! These next twenty-one days are about empowering you to yank the thorny excuses out of your life so that you can thrive as fruitful good soil. While not everyone is called to be an apostle Paul, God has called every Jesus follower to make disciples out of the lost people He's placed in our life. This book will practically take you on a journey to being that person.

Who can you read this book with?

> *Therefore, put on the full armor of God, so that when the day of evil comes, you may be able*

to stand your ground, and after you have done everything, to stand. Stand firm then, with the belt of truth buckled around your waist, with the breastplate of righteousness in place, and with your feet fitted with the readiness that comes from the gospel of peace. In addition to all this, take up the shield of faith, with which you can extinguish all the flaming arrows of the evil one. Take the helmet of salvation and the sword of the Spirit, which is the word of God.

Ephesians 6:13-17

Satan doesn't want you reading this book or putting the scriptures we study into practice. Expect there to be spiritual warfare. So don't read it alone. Look at the context of the whole book of Ephesians, where the image of "the body" is a running theme:

*And God placed all things under his feet and appointed him to be head over everything for the church, which is **his body**, the fullness of him who fills everything in every way.*

Ephesians 1:22, 23

*This mystery is that through the gospel the Gentiles are heirs together with Israel, members together of **one body**, and sharers together in the promise in Christ Jesus.*

Ephesians 3:6

INTRODUCTION

*Instead, speaking the truth in love, we will grow to become in every respect the **mature body** of him who is the head, that is, Christ.*

Ephesians 4:15

Unity of God's people is imperative, perhaps even more so in our fight against spiritual warfare. The armor we know so well wasn't designed merely for a single physical body. It's designed for God's people together. The central way you'll endure Satan's attacks of discouragement, distractions, and doubts is by being deeply united with other believers. If getting a copy of this book for a friend or family member slows you down a day or two, it will be well worth it. We need others for accountability and celebration.

So, before you start this journey, I strongly encourage you to find two groups of people: those who will pray for you daily and those who will join you on the journey.

Take a minute and write down some names of people who you could ask to join you in either of these ways.

People who could pray for me:

_____

_____

_____

People who could read the book with me:

_____

_____

_____

How should you read this?

> *Therefore, everyone who hears these words of mine and puts them into practice is like a wise man who built his house on the rock. The rain came down, the streams rose, and the winds blew and beat against that house; yet it did not fall, because it had its foundation on the rock. But everyone who hears these words of mine and does not put them into practice is like a foolish man who built his house on sand. The rain came down, the streams rose, and the winds blew and beat against that house, and it fell with a great crash.*

Matthew 7:24-27

Jesus ends the Sermon on the Mount with these well-known words. You've sung the song; you've heard the sermons. Tell me, how do we build our house on the rock instead of the sand?

For most of my Christian life, I would have answered that we need to build our lives on Jesus, the rock. If we put our faith in

INTRODUCTION

Him, then we are wise. If we don't, then we're on the sand and our house will come tumbling down. Isn't that how all good little Sunday school boys and girls would answer?

But wait. Read that first verse again. That's not what Jesus is saying here. *"Therefore, everyone who hears these words of mine **and puts them into practice** is like a wise man who built his house on the rock."* **The difference between your house being on the rock and sand is not merely intellectual belief but rather whether I take what I learn from God's Word and put it into practice. Most of us are educated far beyond our levels of obedience. It's time to change that.**

On this journey, you are going to practice obedience. Every day, you will read Scripture and then have a simple daily challenge to put that Scripture into practice. While this book is possible to read in twenty-one days, don't automatically go to the next day until you've obeyed the previous day. Each new day will start with a simple question: How did yesterday's challenge go? If it was a no-go, then don't move forward. If one day is a struggle, read it again—and again—until you master it. This might feel uncomfortable and annoying, but we want to build our house on rock, not sand.

Finally, a word about the author: Excited.

Dear Jesus, transform us into the disciple makers that you have made each of us to be. Change us from the inside out and blow us away with all You have in store. In Jesus Name, Amen.

DAY 1

the habits of a disciple maker

Expectations are always good to deal with up front. Over these next twenty-one days, what are we after? What's the goal? The title of this book kind of speaks for itself. It would be a misrepresentation not to lay out a plan on how you could be a disciple maker in three weeks, but that should beg the question:

What is a disciple maker?

The obvious answer is simple: "one who has made at least one disciple." (Wow, this book really starts in the deep end.)

The problem is that we are not really in control of when that happens.

Jesus said to his disciples who he had been pouring into for more than three years, "I am the vine; you are the branches. If you remain in me and I in you, you will bear much fruit; apart from me you can do nothing" (John 15:5).

My friend Vance Pitman says we often think that verse says that apart from Jesus we can't do big things. That gives us too much credit. Jesus clearly communicates that apart from him we can do *nothing*. We've got no chance to produce *anything*. Bad news: that means we can't make disciples—on our own. Good news: we're not on our own.

Jesus's role is to bring the fruit; our job is simply to stay connected to him.

A few minutes later Jesus says again, "You did not choose me, but I chose you and appointed you so that you might go and bear fruit—fruit that will last—and so that whatever you ask in my name the Father will give you" (John 15:16).

If Jesus chose you and me to make disciples, then he's the one calling the shots on when and where it will happen. Our role as branches is to get as close to him and his teaching as possible and then hold on for dear life.

As much as we would like to feel like God is obligated to reward us with life-changing ministry simply because we picked up this book, He's not. Twenty-one days from now, God may or may not bring someone into your life to disciple. (Sorry if you were hoping for some kind of money-back guarantee.)

With that said, let's go back to our definition of disciple maker. Here is a better working definition: One who daily lives out disciple-making habits in their life.

James Cleary says in his best-selling book, *Atomic Habits*, "You should be far more concerned with your current trajectory than with your current results." Later in the book he adds, "When you fall in love with the process rather than the product, you don't have to wait to give yourself permission to be happy."

DAY 1: THE HABITS OF A DISCIPLE MAKER

So, whether or not you're standing in a pool watching an inspiring baptism in twenty-one days, if you live out what you learn in this book, you will become the kind of person Jesus uses to transform lives.

Remember in the introduction how I was talking about what it takes to build your house on the rock? Each day we will end with a challenge for you to live out. To build on the rock you must put Jesus's words into practice. Some may take a few minutes (like today's), and some will require longer as you build a new daily habit in your life. These challenges are responses to Scripture, and they will make you more like Jesus, the ultimate disciple maker.

I've had many people smarter than me explain it like a sailboat. Only God can bring the wind, but we need to learn *how* to raise the sails and, more importantly, develop the *habits* of keeping them up. Then when the Holy Spirit moves, we are able to go farther and faster. That may seem mundane on some days, but on other days it enables God to take us on the ride of our lives.

This has sure been true for me in my journey to becoming a disciple maker. I'd been a pastor for nineteen years, and it was all going really well . . . until God threw a grenade into the middle of it.

My family lived in a house that overlooked a park. Over the years God would periodically wake me up in the middle of the night with a clear instruction to get out of bed and go down to the park to await a word from Him.

In the spring of 2018 I had one of those middle-of-the-night encounters with God. As I stood in my long-sleeve T-shirt in the frigid San Diego weather, I heard God say to me word for word,

"Jim, I love the story of your church. **(We were four years old, baptizing a lot of people and starting to plant other churches as well.)**

BUT . . . **(uh-oh)**

You've missed the whole point. I called you to make disciples that make disciples and YOU'RE NOT."

The voice wasn't audible, but it could not have been more clear. It hit me like a ton of bricks and instinctively I wanted to push back.

What do you mean we're not making disciples that make disciples? Look at how many new believers we've had. What about all the people we've baptized? We're doing SO much better than most other—

Oh. I realized who I was trying to argue with and sat down and tried to process through all the implications of God's message to me. Which led me down a path not unlike the one I lay out in this book.

My journey has not been smooth or without doubts and detours, but it has led me to an excitement in my faith that I'd never experienced before. And it all started with an acknowledgement—a confession, even—that I needed to grow in the area of disciple making. If you believe that for yourself, you are right where you need to be to start this journey.

DAY 1: THE HABITS OF A DISCIPLE MAKER

Day One Challenge

Simply desiring to want to grow as a disciple maker is a wonderful first step that most Christians never slow down enough to contemplate. You've started that journey. Congratulations! But make no mistake, Satan does not want you to turn this into a lifestyle. Cultivate the habit of carving out dedicated time to grow by committing to a specific time and place that you will read a chapter in this book each day.

I will read every day until I finish this book:

When: _____

Where: _____

DAY 2

disciple making versus discipleship

How did yesterday's challenge go? (That you're reading this is a good sign!)

From my experience, when most people hear the word discipleship, they think of a program within a church or ministry to help Christians mature in their faith. This is a great thing! I am 100 percent pro-discipleship, and my walk with Jesus has been strengthened because of it. That you're reading this book, I'll assume you agree with me. Let's all shout together, "Discipleship is awesome!"

Here's my one concern, though. For all the Christians who support the idea of discipleship programs, there are embarrassingly few new disciples being made. Jesus's last words in the Great Commission are well known, but we seem to be missing the point.

> *All authority in heaven and on earth has been given to me. Therefore go and make disciples of all nations, baptizing them in the name of the Father and of the Son and of the Holy Spirit, and teaching them to obey everything*

DAY 2: DISCIPLE MAKING VERSUS DISCIPLESHIP

I have commanded you. And surely I am with you always, to the very end of the age.

Matthew 28:18-20

Here are three simple takeaways from these verses that I used to miss:

Disciple Making Is Not Optional for Jesus Followers

"Therefore go . . ." While Jesus is speaking to specific people in a specific time, the implication of his message applies to all of his followers at all times. Jesus isn't *inviting* us to join him in his ministry, he's *commanding* us. This isn't a graduate-level assignment for the best of the best Christians. This is a basic component of what it means to follow him. And yet somehow, Christians find ways to discuss and pick apart this passage until it has lost its power and urgency. As a parent, when I tell my kids, "I am your father, therefore go and clean your room," I'm not looking for contemplation; I'm looking for a clean room. I don't want them to watch Marie Kondo for hours figuring out how to clean their room. I don't want them to gather and talk about how wise and worthy I am for desiring a clean room. I don't want them to convince themselves that I'm talking about their siblings who are naturally gifted at cleaning. No, I just want obedience.

Jesus also desires obedience. His words make it clear that you can't be a disciple without being a disciple maker. Unfortunately, somewhere along the way we have separated the two. For Jesus they are one and the same.

Disciple Making Starts before New Disciples Believe

There are three commands Jesus gives here. Go make disciples of all nations, baptize these disciples, and teach them to obey all the stuff Jesus has taught you to obey.

Jesus was sending them to the nations. The nations had never heard of Jesus before. If disciple-making was simply helping Christians grow in their faith, they would have had no one to disciple. This is important: the disciple making process had to begin before it resulted in a saving faith in Christ.

And then they were to baptize them. In the book of Acts how long did new believers wait to get baptized? We read over and over that their baptism happened that same day. For example, when Philip went to Samaria, he spent time with them preaching. And then, "when they believed Philip as he proclaimed the good news of the kingdom of God and the name of Jesus Christ, they were baptized, both men and women" (Acts 8:12). When Jesus instructs us to go make disciples, the assumption is that we find those who don't know him and *along the way,* as we pour into them, they will surrender their lives to Christ. At that point we are called to baptize them immediately and then continue to disciple them by helping them obey all of Jesus's teachings. But disciple making *starts* with unbelievers.

Around the world today in places where the gospel is exploding, the phrase "disciple to conversion" is often used. This is the disciple-making process that you will begin practicing over the next three weeks, as you start intentionally engaging spiritually with your unsaved friends, relatives, neighbors, co-workers long before they will be able to articulate that you're discipling them.

DAY 2: DISCIPLE MAKING VERSUS DISCIPLESHIP

Disciple Making Must Produce More Disciple Makers

Notice Jesus doesn't tell us to merely teach others but to "[teach] them *to obey everything*." Obedience is way harder than knowledge alone, and we will dive deeper into this later. For now, let's just pause at the first practical application of this command. Surely this commission to make disciples is included in the list of obeying everything he'd commanded. Which infers that Jesus is not merely calling us to make disciples; he's commanding us to make disciple makers. Therefore, the true evidence of whether we are following the Great Commission is found not in whether we make disciples but whether our disciples are making disciples.

When I first discovered this, it was incredibly convicting. After decades of following Jesus, my list of people I'd personally discipled was long. But when I contemplated how many of my disciples had then gone on to make disciples themselves, it was disheartening. When I pressed further, looking one more generation into my disciples making disciples that make disciples, it was nearly nonexistent.

And yet, in the parts of the world where movements are exploding, disciples making disciples that make disciples is natural. Third generation and beyond is where exponential growth happens.

At this point you may be thinking, *Thanks! This is even harder than I thought.*

But I think that's the point. Apart from Him we can do nothing. Jesus promised that He would help us and be with us to the very end of the age. We will talk about that more tomorrow.

Day Two Challenge

Spend a few minutes answering these questions and then praying over the answers.

1. Who helped make you a disciple? Pre-conversion? Post-conversion?

2. Who have you discipled and baptized?

3. Have any of the people you discipled gone on to disciple others? Who?

DAY 3

doubts and authority

How did yesterday's challenge go? Does it make you want to keep going and learn how to do this better? Since you're reading today, I hope so!

It's always helpful to know the context. I've got a bad habit of falling asleep at inconvenient times during movies. Years ago, I was at a theater watching a Tom Cruise film with some friends. As we walked out they raved about the film, but I complained that the main character kept on changing his personality and it was bad screenwriting. They asked, "Are you talking about the main guy or his clone?" There was a clone??? That explained a lot! Context is helpful.

As a high-school student many years ago, I memorized the verses we studied yesterday—what I thought was the whole Great Commission. But did you know that there's more to it? Open your Bible right now to Matthew 28. Where does the heading "Great Commission" start?

Most modern translations begin two verses before Jesus starts talking. Check it out:

> *Then the eleven disciples went to Galilee, to the mountain where Jesus had told them to go. When they saw him, they worshipped him; but*

some doubted. Then Jesus came to them and said ...

Matthew 28: 16-18

The Great Commission is for all of us, but it was spoken to real people, in a real place and time. The context of Jesus's famous words brings to light two important truths about disciple making for all of us that we can't miss.

Jesus Gave the Great Commission to Worshipers and Doubters!

The disciples showed up at the mountain Jesus had instructed them to go to. It says they worshipped Jesus. And yet we read, "but some doubted." Their obedience and response convey that their doubts were not about His resurrection or identity. They were wavering with their own insecurities. In fact, the only other time this Greek word for *doubt* is used in the New Testament is when Peter walks on the water to Jesus and then wavers and Jesus asks him, "Why did you doubt?"

Why did they still feel insecure? Well, for starters, Jesus's idea of being Messiah wasn't quite what they were expecting. Some of them were still hoping Jesus was going to kick the Romans out of Israel. And they probably had a lot of the same insecurities we have today: I can't do this ... I'm too young ... this is too different ... I've made too many mistakes... What will my family think? ...

So, some still doubted, but notice what is *not* said. "Then Jesus turned only to the worshipers and said . . ." No, Jesus looked at the worshippers–*and doubters*–and delivered the Great Commission. For us, that means that our doubts are NOT an acceptable excuse for not making disciples. It also means Jesus sees way more in us than we have ever seen in ourselves.

The Disciples' First Obedience Step Was Showing Up at This Mountain in Galilee

In your opinion, which was a harder command for the disciples to obey: Going to meet their beloved resurrected Jesus away from the heat of recent events in Jerusalem? Or going and making disciples of all nations in places they would never wish to go?

Doesn't step one seem a whole lot easier? And yet, isn't this exactly how Jesus works? As we take a step of faith, he reveals a new step and then another one and another. This is the reason I wrote this short book with only one challenge a day. Baby steps can lead to life change.

With this context, the next verse now makes more sense: "All authority in heaven and earth has been given to me . . ." which implies that He's now passing it on to them—and us. Now consider how many times Jesus played the "God card" in his public ministry to claim authority over everything. Never! This is it. He clearly claims his authority here for the purpose of inspiring and empowering his disciples to go make more disciples. Jesus' plan to reach the world includes self-identified doubters because He knows our ability to make disciples is not about our self-assurance but His authority in us. And if that authority wasn't enough, Jesus's last line is a resounding echo: ". . . and surely I'll be with you to the very end of the age." We have his authority to go out and make disciples. And we also have his very presence with us. That is more than enough to overcome our doubts.

So, let's deal with our doubts. You may not have as much fruit as Rick Warren, but God has intentionally put you in relationships and given you His own authority to make disciples out of those who are far from God.

Day Three Challenge

Here is a list of doubts Christians consciously or subconsciously carry around that prevent them from attempting to disciple people into a relationship with Jesus, baptizing them and helping them become disciple makers. Circle the ones you most identify with.

- I don't know enough.
- I'm too shy.
- Disciple making isn't my spiritual gift.
- I'm too new in my faith.
- If you knew my past.
- I'm too busy.
- I can't take rejection.
- No one discipled me.
- I don't know any non-Christians.
- My church hasn't taught me.
- I'm just not comfortable with this.
- I'm too young.
- I'm too old.
- None of my Christians friends do this.
- Fill in the blank with your own: _____

DAY 3: DOUBTS AND AUTHORITY

Now spend time praying this prayer over every doubt:

Dear Jesus, although I carry the doubt of _____, I realize that you STILL call me to be a disciple maker. I claim your authority and lean on your presence. Be strong in me to overcome this doubt and replace it with great faith.

HABIT #1

PRAYING FOR SOMEONE TO DISCIPLE

(DAYS 4 THROUGH 7)

DAY 4

pray for yourself

The first habit of a disciple maker is prayer. Prayer is not what you do *before* the work, prayer *is* the work. Extraordinary prayer is at the center of every movement of God happening around the world.

I recently was speaking to a disciple-making friend in India who sees supernatural healings that turn into salvations and, ultimately, churches—on a weekly basis. I asked him about his prayer life, and he humbly shared that he's up by 4 a.m. *every* morning to spend his first two hours with God.

Before we all get overwhelmed or overly convicted by our passion for pushing the snooze button being greater than our passion for prayer, let me define what extraordinary prayer is. It's simply extra-ordinary prayer. If you rarely pray except before some meals or at church, and you grow to spending five focused minutes talking with God every day, that is extra-ordinary—more than ordinary—prayer for you. If you currently spend five minutes a day praying for people, but over the next few weeks it transforms into ten to fifteen minutes a day, then that would be extra-ordinary prayer for you. If you tend to be haphazard and easily distracted in your prayers, but through this book helps you implement a focused, intentional prayer routine, that is extraordinary prayer! No matter where you are at, you can do this! God meets us where we are at and celebrates our steps of faith.

Paul wrote a lot of letters to the churches he helped plant, and at some point, he usually asked his brothers and sisters to pray for him. Look at how Paul wanted to be prayed for.

> *Pray also for me, that whenever I speak, words may be given me so that I will fearlessly make known the mystery of the gospel.*

Ephesians 6:19

> *And pray for us, too, that God may open a door for our message, so that we may proclaim the mystery of Christ, for which I am in chains. Pray that I may proclaim it clearly, as I should.*

Colossians 4:3, 4

> *As for other matters, brothers and sisters, pray for us that the message of the Lord may spread rapidly and be honored, just as it was with you.*

2 Thessalonians 3:1

Paul's most popular prayer request was boldness in proclaiming the gospel (so that he could make disciples). If that's what the greatest missionary to ever walk the planet prayed for, how much more so should we?

If anyone ever asks you how they can pray for you, learn to say, "Pray for me to grow as a disciple maker." From my experience,

DAY 4: PRAY FOR YOURSELF

the most popular prayer requests Christians usually share are centered around health and safety. That's not a bad thing, but if you want to be an obedient disciple maker, it's time to pray like one.

And then, pray for yourself this way. This chapter is not titled "Getting other people to pray for you." While having prayer support is vital, it is hypocritical if you're not praying for yourself what you're asking others to pray for you.

Here are some examples of other powerful disciple-making prayers:

- Open my eyes to truly see the people around me.
- Open my eyes to see the needs of others.
- Open my eyes to see where you're already working.
- Open my eyes to see the harvest—those whose hearts are open to God.
- Cross my path with someone who needs you and is ready to listen to you.
- Give me boldness to initiate spiritual conversations.
- Guide me in the words to say.
- Help _____ (you fill in the blank)

If you only have thirty seconds in your daily schedule to live this out, start with this simple disciple-making prayer:

Jesus, use me to disciple someone into a relationship with You, to baptize them and then to get out of the way and watch them baptize others.

Praying that prayer will change your life. Read it over again.

Notice, it is simply praying that you would actually live out the Great Commission. Might that be the kind of prayer request God would want to answer emphatically?

Haven't you found that your passion often follows your prayers? The things you pray fervently about, you begin to feel more passionate about, and then you begin to see more and more of God's answers. I'm currently writing this chapter in my swimsuit, because in a few minutes, I'll be driving to the beach to watch a young man—who I discipled into a relationship with Jesus and baptized—now baptize several of his friends and family members. I've prayed a long time for this. It never gets old.

Day Four Challenge

Pray the following prayer for yourself today. And then continue praying it daily for the rest of your life:

Jesus, use me to disciple someone into a relationship with You, to baptize them and then to get out of the way and watch them baptize others.

DAY 5

pray for others

How did yesterday's challenge go? If you've not prayed for yourself as a disciple maker yet today, then take a minute to do that now.

In addition to praying for ourselves, we must raise our commitment, strategy and habits in regards to how we pray for the people God has placed in our lives. Before I approach people about God, I need to approach God about these people.

This probably isn't a shock to anyone. Yes, I know as a Jesus follower that I'm supposed to pray for others. Jesus's own brother said, "Confess your sins to each other AND PRAY FOR EACH OTHER so that you may be healed. The prayers of righteous person are POWERFUL and EFFECTIVE" (James 5:16).

As disciple makers, we must pray for others in a spontaneous *and* scheduled way. Absolutely we must listen to the small voice of the Holy Spirit when He brings people to the forefront of our minds to pray for. For example, a friend in Africa recently woke up in the middle of the night with me on his mind. He spent time praying and then called (it was early evening here). God used this spontaneous prayer as a huge encouragement to me as I was seeking God's wisdom on something.

But if we ONLY pray for people spontaneously, we likely won't pray enough. I am a self-professed expert at getting challenged to do something—and then doing nothing about it. I'll hear a message on Sunday and be totally convicted, but by Tuesday I won't even remember what the sermon was about . . . and I was the one preaching. Most of us have the desire to pray for people, but if you're anything like me, we often fall short on the execution. I've had to repent for my overuse of the prayer emoji! Anyone with me? You type those little hands and then forget to ever spend more time praying intentionally for the person?

As disciple makers who know we can do nothing apart from God, we must also come up with a plan to pray for people. There are a million ways to do this but I'm going to share with you what I do. On the next page is simple worksheet where you are going to write out names of people God has placed in your life. Be quiet before God and ask him to guide your mind and pen as you fill it out. If you don't have enough names to fill in all the blanks, that's fine. And if you need to add extra, that's cool, too.

It would be overwhelming for most of us to pray for every person every day, so tomorrow we will talk more about how to turn these lists into a daily habit. With just a few extra minutes a day of focused intentional prayer, in the course of a year you will have spent hours in "effective prayer" and experience abundant answers.

Now, from personal experience, it's still easy to make this monotonous if we simply run through the names praying vaguely for God to bless them and keep them safe. To keep it fresh, God's Word is packed with amazing prayers we can use to

DAY 5: PRAY FOR OTHERS

grow our hearts for the lost people He's placed in our lives and empower us to step out.

Here are some examples:

- Ephesians 1:17, 18
- Ephesians 3:16–19
- Philippians 1:9–12
- 1 Thessalonians 3:12, 13
- 2 Thessalonians 1:11, 12
- 2 Thessalonians 3:5
- 1 Peter 3:8
- Colossians 3:15
- Hebrews 6:11, 12
- Hebrews 12:1, 2
- Psalm 119:18
- Psalm 86:11

For example, for an entire week I use Ephesians 1:17, 18 and pray for each person that God would give them wisdom and revelation to know God better and know the hope to which He has called them. The following week I'm using 1 Peter 3:8 and praying that each person would be like-minded, sympathetic, loving, compassionate and humble.

Disciple makers have the habit of praying for themselves daily. They also have the habit of praying for others spontaneously and systematically. Check it out, less than one week in and you're already becoming a disciple maker.

Day Five Challenge
(The FRANCE sheet)

Take five minutes and ask God to guide your mind as you fill in the blanks below with names. You can write down people who are Christians and non-Christians. Pick one (or more) people to pray for today.

Friends _____ _____ _____

_____ _____ _____

Relatives _____ _____ _____

_____ _____ _____

Acquaintances (mail carrier, teachers, etc.) _____

_____ _____ _____

Neighbors _____ _____ _____

_____ _____ _____

Co-workers/Classmates _____ _____

_____ _____ _____

Earlier in life _____ _____ _____

_____ _____ _____

Permission to copy this form for your ministerial use.

DAY 6

praying with others

How did yesterday's challenge go? Have you spent a few minutes praying for yourself as a disciple maker and for one of the groups from your FRANCE sheet you filled out yesterday?

Prayer is not only what we do before disciple making, it's also one of the best transitions into a disciple-making relationship. Let me introduce you to my wife's favorite disciple-making tool, what we call the Prayer Calendar. This prayer calendar concept was created by David and Paul Watson. They are amazing disciple-making coaches and authors of the book *Contagious Disciple Making*. If you follow *all* their steps I describe here, you'll create a daily habit that can bridge the gap from prayer into a disciple-making relationship.

While I am a flaming extrovert who derives great joy from walking up to total strangers and engaging them in spiritual conversations, my wife is the complete opposite. Talking even to friends exhausts her, so she struggled with how she was supposed to make disciples without completely withering. Until we learned this strategy. Now she has our kids' friends' moms, PTA moms, soccer and basketball team moms, Bunko ladies, neighbors, and Walmart employees on her calendar, and she is regularly engaging in fantastic spiritual conversations that start naturally in response to her praying with them using the Prayer Calendar.

Are you ready for this tool?

Step 1: Fill out the Prayer Calendar (at the end of this chapter)

Assuming you filled out the FRANCE sheet yesterday—(if you didn't, stop! Remember, don't move forward until you complete each step)—this is going to be a piece of cake. Simply transfer the names on that sheet onto your calendar. Put one name in each of the thirty days of the calendar. If you don't have thirty names yet, don't worry. God is good at adding people to your list as you grow in this habit! If you have more than thirty names, you can skip some or double them up. (I'm now up to five names on most of my days, thanks to God continuing to add people to my life who need regular prayer!) Your days can be completely random, or you can try to keep it organized, like lining up yesterday's categories to keep it simple. For example, put all your Friends on Mondays, your Relatives on Tuesdays, Acquaintances on Wednesdays, etc.

Step 2: Contact the person who is on today's date

Once your calendar is filled out, start praying! Like, right now. Find today's date and reach out to the person written on that day. For example, if today is the 11th, reach out to the person you wrote in for the 11th on your calendar.

Reach out to them whatever way is most comfortable for you. You can call them. You can talk to them in person. You can text them. You can message them through social media (as long as

DAY 6: PRAYING WITH OTHERS

you don't get distracted by it!). I personally send them a simple text: "Hey _ _ _ _ _ _ _ _, you are on my prayer calendar today. How specifically can I pray for you today?" Or you could tell them, "I'm trying to start a new habit of intentionally reaching out to and praying for people in my life. How are you doing, and what can I pray for you for?" It's not a bad idea to mix it up from month to month, so that it sounds fresh and personal.

So, go do that right now, before you move on to Step 3. Walk next door or call or text the person RIGHT NOW and find out how you can pray for them. (Unless you're reading this in the middle of the night . . . then you can wait a few hours.)

Step 3: Actually pray *with* them

After they respond with a request, pray with them. That means send back a text or voice note or call them or pray for them in person. A friend who put me on her prayer calendar was struggling with this—calling in person felt too hard, but tendonitis in her thumbs makes it hard for her to text much. But she already kept a prayer journal, so we suggested that she journal out her prayer and then take a picture of the page and text that. This worked well for her, and every month, it's a highlight to see her handwritten note—it's like the novelty of handwritten mail these days!

Now you may be feeling that you'll just skip this part. It feels a little awkward. You can just tell them that you're praying for them.

DON'T SKIP THIS STEP!!!

This part is crucial; it's what turns this tool from a prayer habit to a disciple-making habit. It's so important that if they respond back to you while you're still reading, I give you permission to put the book down and get on your phone . . . only to pray with them! Not to get distracted!

And then, after writing your prayer to them or praying with them aloud, keep them in your thoughts before the Lord throughout the rest of the day.

Now, what if they don't respond? Erase them from your contacts. They are dead to you!

JUST KIDDING!!! DON'T DO THAT!!! If they don't respond to your offer, pray for them on your own. Remember those Bible verses I listed yesterday? Those can be perfect for these situations. Now, if they don't respond two or three months in a row, maybe ask God if you should take them off. Maybe their heart just isn't ready for this yet but will be in the future. God knows. If you can, replace them with another name that you didn't have space for before.

And that's it. That's the prayer calendar. It may seem too basic, but think for a moment, if this became a daily habit in your life, what types of things might happen? I sat down with some friends who were using the prayer calendar, and as a group, we immediately rattled off a long list.

Here were a few we mentioned:

- People would be encouraged. (It's amazing when you reach out to them at just the right time!)

DAY 6: PRAYING WITH OTHERS

- Prayers get answered. (Everyone's faith grows!)
- You grow closer to the person. (Their requests deepen over the months.)
- They get inspired to start the habit themselves. (Multiplication!)
- They ask how they can pray for you. (You get prayed for!)
- You grow as a pray-er. (Writing out a prayer requires more intentionality from you than the prayer emoji!)
- It will inspire spiritual conversations. (People are more open to God when they are struggling.)

One of my friends was not sold on the prayer calendar but was willing to try. With low expectations, he reached out to a longtime friend who had never had interest in spiritual things before. His friend replied asking for prayer for his marriage. My friend texted back a simple but heartfelt prayer, and within minutes his friend called back, deeply moved. He said others had said they were praying for him over the years, but he had never actually heard someone pray for him before. He couldn't believe my friend would talk to God on his behalf like that. He was immediately open to talking about God.

Over the past three days I've given you three different daily prayer habits: pray *for yourself* as a disciple maker, pray *for others* and pray *with* others. Praying for yourself can take less than a minute a day, and praying for and with others can be combined into a few dedicated minutes up front and then a more intentional mindset throughout the day. Make these three simple habits a part of your daily rhythm for at least the next fifteen days, and I believe you will be pleasantly surprised by the spiritual fruit God grows. Continue it for the rest of your life, and you'll be blown away by the results.

Day Six Challenge

You just did it!

DAY 6: PRAYING WITH OTHERS

PRAYER CALENDAR

https://www.youtube.com/watch?v=9zunEXAeh7o

"Every Movement of God starts with a prayer movement. We can't just encourage prayer...we must mobilize it!

Step 1: Write out 30 names of people you know (Ex. cell phone, FB, etc) and then put their name in the top of each box.

Step 2: Reach out to the person 1-2 days in advance and tell them they are on your prayer calendar that day. Ask how you can specifically be praying for them?

Step 3: Either by phone call or text actually pray for them on that day. Have their request on your mind throughout the day.

Step 4: Do this everyday. If you find after 2 months someone doesn't respond then replace them. Keep track of answers prayers.

Step 5: After living this out consistently for at least a few weeks invite and train 2-5 other people to make their own prayer calendar. Ask them how it's going and challenge them to invite/train 2-5 others.

1	2	3	4	5	6	7
8	9	10	11	12	13	14
15	16	17	18	19	20	21
22	23	24	25	26	27	28
29	30	31				

Month 1: Just me! I pray for 30 people or 2 1/2 hours

Month 2: Me and 5 others: 180 people prayed for or 15 hours

Month 3: Me and 25 others: 780 people prayed for or 65 hours

Permission to copy this form for your ministerial use.

DAY 7

celebrating stories and steps of faith

On the last day of each week on this journey, I will share one of my friend's stories about their journey of becoming a multiplying disciple maker. This is Joleene's story:

"As our family of four (with two young kids) moved into our new neighborhood, we prayed God would lead us to the right house where we could be a light among our neighbors. We looked for ways to show love to our neighbors. Our kids baked cookies and delivered them to those on our street. We hosted front yard BBQs and potlucks to try to get to know the people God had placed around us.

"As I started to meet the other women, I shared about my faith and several unbelievers expressed interest in studying the Bible together. Another friend shared with me about this amazing resource called Discovery Bible Study that enabled us to just read the Bible and ask some simple questions. I also started getting some coaching from a great ministry called Contagious Disciple Making that helped me each step of the way.

"One night our little group was studying Leviticus (of all places), and one of the women started connecting the dots between the

DAY 7: CELEBRATING STORIES AND STEPS OF FAITH

sacrificial system and what she had heard about the cross. She desperately wanted to know if the connections she was making from the story were correct. Others in the group began having 'aha' moments as well. I affirmed that she was making the right connections between the two biblical events. She then said that she wanted Jesus to be the sacrifice for her sins and repented and believed. Another woman in the group said that she too wanted to make this step of faith as well. So, two ladies decided to follow Jesus that night.

"Over time, through studying the Bible together, each of the women decided to make Jesus their Lord and Savior. We studied several passages about baptism together, and they all decided to get baptized. That's when the spiritual warfare got very real, and one at a time, they all backed down from taking this faith step. Months went by and we were still meeting weekly. One of the women had a pool built in her backyard and I prayed, 'God is this the open door to bring up baptism again?' I had lots of friends praying and fasting as I called each of the women on the phone. Miraculously, all three said yes, on their own, that they were ready to obey.

The night before the baptism, one woman shared she was having all kinds of panic attacks and crazy dreams about her past. She was in tears as I explained spiritual warfare to her and prayed over her. I told her, 'The enemy knows that God is going to use you in such powerful ways and doesn't want you to take this step of obedience.'

"The baptism night was absolutely incredible. All their families came to support their wives and moms. We had kids lined on the side of the pool cheering. As I was about to baptize one of the women I asked, 'What is your hope and prayer for the future?' She said, 'I want to grow in relationship with Christ through my prayer life, and I want to share the gospel with people.'

"That act of baptism was like a spiritual transaction that took place for each of them AND for their families that were watching. The presence of the Lord was there in my neighbor's backyard. Afterward, a daughter of one of the women came up to me and said, 'I want to give my life to Jesus and be baptized too.' A short time later, a bunch of the neighbor kids were in the pool practicing baptizing each other.

"One of the ladies I baptized that night now meets with her sister and mother and does a Discovery Bible Study with them. God has opened many other doors to spiritual conversations in our neighborhood since.

"Now, if my story makes it sound like it's all been easy, that couldn't be further from the truth. It's been long and often felt like we were moving backwards. But experiencing a night like that inspired me and my family to see that there is no greater joy than joining Jesus in giving our lives to making disciples. We can't wait to see what's next!"

DAY 7: CELEBRATING STORIES AND STEPS OF FAITH

Day Seven Challenge

Looking back on your first week, spend a few minutes writing down insights you've learned, steps of faith you've taken, and stories of how God is transforming you and transforming others through you. Paul said to the church in Philippi, "Rejoice in the Lord always, again I say rejoice." I think he could have just said, "Celebrate everything." What can you celebrate this week?

HABIT #2

ENGAGING WITH POTENTIAL DISCIPLES

(DAYS 8 THROUGH 11)

DAY 8

living with a mission mindset

How's it going with your prayer calendar? Any stories to celebrate so far?

Kyle grew up going to church, but when he was in fifth grade, his parents got divorced and it felt like the church abandoned him. Twenty-five years later the hurt isn't fresh anymore, but church isn't something he has any interest in. He needs God, but how is he supposed to meet him?

Unfortunately, modern church culture often doesn't help much. Consider this: we have turned the lost person into the missionary. If someone wants to "find God" they need to be the ones who leave their comfort zones and go to a place they've never been, interact with people who are different from them, and do a bunch of things that all seem foreign to them. But Jesus clearly tells his disciples that *we* are the ones who are called to go. We are the ones who are supposed to leave our comfort zones, step into other people's lives, and meet them where they are at.

For the next few days of our journey, we will press into how we can do that better. The first step is living with a mission mindset.

God has intentionally placed you in your neighborhood, workplace, school, kids' sports teams, and other rhythms of life, and he wants to use you there. The Greek word in the New Testament used for this is called *oikos*. It's your natural network of people who you do life with. You probably filled up your prayer calendar with people in your oikos. However, vital question: how many of those people are already Jesus followers?

To live with a mission mindset we need to make some small, but potentially difficult, shifts in how we prioritize our time and how we view where we live, work, and play. We may need to sacrifice some of the time we spend in our Christian bubble and grow in the art of engaging with lost people and meeting them where they are at. We must rearrange our lives to regularly engage with those who don't know Jesus yet. This is the heart of a disciple maker.

Everywhere disciple makers go, they go on mission looking to engage people spiritually. This must be our mindset.

For example, my kids' school is called Mission Meadows Elementary. Meadow is another name for field, right? So, our family calls it our literal Mission Field. We put on the armor of God on our walk to school every morning, complete with hand motions and sound effects. We end with asking, "What are we going to do today?" Our kids shout back, "Show God's love." Then we talk through who they think they'll show God's love to that day and how they'll do it.

My wife substitutes at the school and serves on the PTA to intentionally partner with our kids in reaching the school. As I've mentioned before, she and I have pretty opposite personalities.

DAY 8: LIVING WITH A MISSION MINDSET

I've never met a stranger and she thinks I'm really strange. But introversion doesn't stop her from making disciples. By intentionally engaging with other parents, she's currently meeting with five other moms who are interested in discovering truth about God with her.

Anyone else love the convenience of Walmart grocery pickup? We've made it a point to engage the person bringing out the groceries in friendly conversation and remembering them the next time they serve us. (When we're really good, we try to schedule the same pick-up time each week to increase the likelihood of seeing them again.) Usually we ask if there's any way we can pray for them on the drive home. My wife connected me with one guy who—after months of these interactions—started opening up, and several years later, he still texts me for prayer when he's struggling. That's living with a mission mindset while grocery shopping.

Remember Kyle from the beginning? He's become a friend of mine. Our kids ended up on the same basketball team (coincidence?), and over the weeks of hanging out at practices and games, conversations slowly grew deeper. He shared struggles that I knew God could help him with, but he and his family were never going to come to church. But he was open to learning Bible stories with me and has been faithfully teaching them to his family. God is working.

As we learn to engage the lost, it must start with a mission mindset: God has intentionally placed me here, and I may be the closest to a relationship with Jesus that they ever get. God has called me to go and that will require me to step out of my comfort zone, but I know it's SO worth it.

Day Eight Challenge

Go prayer walking around your neighborhood or workplace for at least twenty minutes today. Ask God to give you a mission mindset and do some imagination prayer. What could you imagine God doing there? Write down what God speaks to your mind.

DAY 9

intentional conversations

Did you do your prayer walk? If not, put this book down and live out yesterday's challenge first.

St. Francis of Assisi was an incredibly inspiring Jesus follower, but he didn't actually say his most famous quote. Have you heard it? "Preach the gospel always; use words if necessary." It sounds deep, but even St. Francis knew better than that. My friend Vance Pitman likens this quote to, "Give me your phone number; use digits if necessary." The truth is we shouldn't bother sharing our faith if we're not willing to first show it. But at some point we will need to share with words.

Disciple makers have intentional conversations. I want to share a simple tool that I also learned from Paul Watson and his team at Contagious Disciple Making (ContagiousDiscipleMaking.com). It's called the conversation quadrant, and it will be our focus the next three days. Each day we will walk through easy ways to move a conversation from one quadrant to another.

Casual Conversations	Meaningful Conversations
Discovery Conversations	Spiritual Conversations

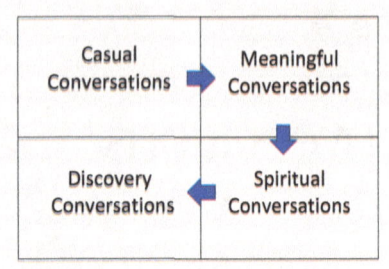

Casual - Surface Talk. Facts
(Ex. The weather, where you're from, age of kids)

Meaningful - Sharing Vulnerably. Feelings
(Ex. Stresses, struggles, passions)

Spiritual - God Talk. Sharing your story.
(Ex. Asking about spiritual background)

Discovery - Informal Bible Study.
Ex. (Sharing a Bible Story and discussing together.)

Unless this is someone you are never going to see again, this process doesn't have to happen all at one time. Also, clearly, this is not a rule, just a resource. But in our mission mindset we should be constantly looking for ways to naturally move conversations toward spiritual and discovery. You might be surprised by how many people are actually quite interested and open!

Moving Conversations to Meaningful

My mom taught me that there are two kinds of people in the world: those who walk around saying, "Here I am!" and those who walk around saying, "There you are!" The secret to moving conversations to meaningful topics is by being others-focused, a "there you are" type person.

Jesus was a pro at this. His emotion that was mentioned over and over before he did miraculous healings was compassion. He identified and brought out the positive qualities in people whom others had missed. He praised the persistence of blind Bartimaeus, he generated the generosity of Zacchaeus, he inspired the influence of the woman at the well. Jesus was also a next-level question asker. He asked 307 questions in the

DAY 9: INTENTIONAL CONVERSATIONS

Gospel accounts. He was asked 183 questions himself but only answered it directly three times. Usually he responded with a story or another question back at the person.

As we try to move conversations to meaningful, we want to identify people's pain points and discern what stresses and struggles are keeping them up at night. Or we want to find what makes them most passionate and gets them up in the morning. Ask good questions. Share your own weakness and ask for their input. Encourage them. Here are some ideas:

> *I'm trying to figure out what to do for _____ . . . What are you most looking forward to about _____?*
>
> *Motherhood/new career/retirement/_____ was so hard for me. How are you doing with it? What are your biggest challenges in this stage of life?*
>
> *If you could have one miracle happen in your life, what would it be?*
>
> *You seem to be really into _____, <u>why</u> is that?*
>
> *You're really good at _____, how did you get that way?*
>
> *Can you tell me about your tattoo? (There is almost always a story.)*

Once you've asked good questions, then be quiet and really listen. Listen for pain points, like challenges in their marriage, family, health, or career. Listen for things you can offer to pray for. Listen for meaningful ways you could serve them. Like . . .

> *"I could pick up your kids after school tomorrow."*
>
> *"I've had some of the same experiences before; would you ever want to get coffee?"*
>
> *"It sounds like you need a break. Our family is going to drop off dinner tomorrow."*
>
> *"I'm putting in my Walmart grocery order right now. What are ten things you need?"*

I was at my daughters' soccer practice recently and simply remarked to another dad that he seemed to be really close with his kids and I wanted to know his secret. Within seconds he was pouring out his story of being a workaholic with failing health and a lot of regrets. He hit rock bottom six months earlier and had started to make drastic changes in his priorities. He then said, I'm trying to find balance in my life physically, relationally, and spiritually. I simply asked, "What does that look like spiritually?" He said, "I've got no idea, I need help on that one." I smiled. (Is it really that easy sometimes?)

DAY 9: INTENTIONAL CONVERSATIONS

Day Nine Challenge

Pick someone in your life that you have only had casual conversations with and use what you learned today to try to move the conversation to Meaningful. For example, knock on a neighbor's door who you don't know very well and bring a plate of cookies. Ask them at least one of the questions you learned today. Or strike up a conversation with another parent at your kid's practice. Or stop by a co-worker's desk and make a positive observation about them, and then ask questions.

DAY 10

moving from meaningful to spiritual conversations

How did it go with your challenge yesterday? Were you able to get into any meaningful conversations with anyone? If not, try again today! Describe your attempt here:

Recently the Surgeon General Advisory called attention to the public health crisis of loneliness, isolation, and lack of connection in our country. There are a lot of people around you who are starving for meaningful relationships.

This morning I grabbed coffee with a seventy-one-year-old guy I just met named Mark. He shared his story about losing his job during the pandemic and having a vivid dream of a T-shirt that simply said, "How can I pray for you?" He'd not had spiritual dreams before but when the dream persisted five days in a row, he had the shirt made and started walking around the downtown area of our city seeing if anyone would take him up on his offer.

Mark shared that he has only missed about twenty days in the last three years since he started and has had more than 2,000 people approach him asking for prayer. At first, he was blown away at the level of transparency people would have with a complete stranger. Now he expects it! He also shared of people running up and throwing their arms around him for a hug shouting, "God answered your prayer. I'm healed!"

You might not have Mark's boldness to talk to thousands of strangers, but you can still experience the power of the simple question on his T-shirt. As you step into meaningful conversations with people and hear about their stresses, struggles, and passions, that question might be the simplest way you can steer the dialogue towards spiritual things.

"Has anyone ever prayed for you about that?"

Right now, practice saying those words out loud.

If there is ANY spiritual interest on their part at all, this simple question will open the door. Some people might decline, but for me, I've found less than a few that have been offended by the offer for prayer. You might get . . .

> *"Well, I'm not really religious."*
>
> *"No, but I could take all the help I can get."*
>
> *"God's too busy to care about my junk."*

But you never know when those hesitations thinly cover a truly hungry heart.

As long as they don't clearly say no, simply ask, "Do you mind if I pray right now?" It doesn't need to be the greatest prayer ever (and definitely not very long), just be authentic and caring. You've now introduced spiritual things in a way that is a blessing to them.

My wife prefers to do this through the "safety" of a text. She will have a meaningful conversation with a fellow mom about a struggle, and then follow up the next day with a text, "I was thinking about our conversation yesterday, and I've been praying for you. I'm praying that _____." Sometimes the most she gets back is "Thank you for the positive thoughts." But most of her discipling relationships came from these texts.

A few years back I started the habit of sending an email to each of my kids' teachers thanking them profusely for pouring their lives into my kids. I end the email with, "I try to pray for the people God's placed in our life who have been a blessing to our family. That definitely includes you. Are there any specific ways I can pray for you?" Every teacher every year has responded, including the ones without spiritual beliefs, and often it has opened further dialogue.

Another way to move from meaningful to spiritual is by serving others and then dripping God into the conversation as the reason why. The key word is dripping, not deluging or dunking.

For example, if you know your co-worker is discouraged at home, you could grab them their favorite Starbucks on your way into the office and simply say, "I woke up this morning just thanking God that I get to work with you." Or if someone asked to borrow your truck you could say, "I told God it's His truck not mine. Of course you can use it . . . any other way I can help?"

The goal is not to forcefully name drop Jesus into the conversation but to just let Jesus drip off your words and actions naturally, showing He's important to you.

DAY 10: MOVING FROM MEANINGFUL TO SPIRITUAL CONVERSATIONS

Here are some other ways you can drip Jesus in conversation naturally:

- Express something you are grateful for and give God credit for it.
- Share about something that God recently taught you.
- Tell about a miracle you've experienced or witnessed.
- Disclose something you're asking God to help you with.
- Describe a trial you went through and how God helped.

One of our best topics for this in our family is our adoption story (and quickly following pregnancy). Any time anyone asks if our girls are twins, or hints at their curiosity about our son being black, we've got a wide-open window to share all about God's hand in bringing us our kids. His fingerprints are all over our story, and so many spiritual conversations have come from our openness.

If the person you are talking to seems extremely uninterested or turned off to spiritual things, that's okay. No need to force it. We are looking for people in whom God is already at work to potentially disciple. At least for now, don't turn the faucet up; it's okay to turn it off. A leaky drip can be pretty annoying. And God has a habit of bringing people back around when they are ready.

Day Ten Challenge

Attempt to have an intentional conversation with someone in your life that moves from meaningful to spiritual. Ideally (although it doesn't have to be) it could be the person you had a meaningful conversation with yesterday. A great follow up could be, "I was thinking about what you said yesterday. Have you ever had someone pray for you about that?"

DAY 11

moving from spiritual to discovery conversations

How did yesterday's challenge go? Were you able to move a conversation to spiritual? If not, try again today. Write down your experience here:

___
___
___
___
___
___
___
___

People love stories. I'm no different. I was a screenwriting major in college and have seen the power in sharing a compelling story. So did Jesus. He told more than fifty stories throughout the Gospels, and it was one of his main go-to strategies to help people grow in their faith.

In Luke 10, an expert in the law approaches Jesus with a question about eternal life. Jesus cleverly responds with two questions of his own. "What is written in the law? How do you read it?" The law expert quotes Scripture, and Jesus tells him he nailed the pop quiz. The man comes back with another question. "Who is my neighbor?" Again, Jesus doesn't answer but responds with a story about a Jewish man receiving love from a hated Samaritan and, surprise! It ends with one more question that would give the man the answer he was after.

Why doesn't Jesus just give theologically accurate answers to the man's questions? He obviously knew the answer and could have probably saved some time. I'm sure there are many answers but here are two main ones. Jesus knew . . .

1. Good stories can be insightful and unassuming.
2. A message DISCOVERED is much more powerful than a message DELIVERED.

Today we are talking about moving from dripping God into a spiritual conversation to finding opportunities where you can help people who are far from God discover truths about Him. In getting to know them you've discussed some of their stresses, struggles, and passions. You've applied yesterday's lesson and brought God naturally into your story . . . and maybe even prayed for them in what they are dealing with.

DAY 11: MOVING FROM SPIRITUAL TO DISCOVERY CONVERSATIONS

It's obviously important to continue praying for them. Ask God to reveal a biblical story related to what they are facing. Then reach out to them again and say something like,

"I was thinking about what you're going through this past week and a story came to mind that I think would encourage you. Can I share it with you?"

Now, before you decide that you could never say something like that, think about it. Aren't these some of the nicest words someone could say to you? "I was thinking of you." At this point it's rare to find someone who turns down your offer to share a story, especially since you thought of it specifically for them.

You may not have told Bible stories since you were a little kid in Sunday school, so here are a couple tips in sharing a first story with someone:

Share the story in your own words. You totally don't need it memorized, but study the story a few times to remember as many details as possible.

Share a story that's easy to understand and discuss. All Scripture is God-breathed and profitable, but every passage is not necessarily equally relatable to every situation.

Finally, share a story that's applicable to what they are going through. For example, if someone shares about something difficult they need to do, you could share Matthew 14:22-33 where Jesus invites Peter to walk on water.

After you've shared the story, assuming they seem to be listening, then follow it up with . . .

- What do you learn from this story?
- How could you apply this story to your life/what you're going through?

Remember a message discovered is more powerful than a message delivered. You don't need to tell them what they should get out of the story. Allow God's Spirit to lead them. It's okay not to bring up every insight you've learned over the years. You didn't know the details of the Sea of Galilee's weather patterns or the Greek word for *faith* when you first heard the story. They don't need to know it either. Keep it simple and let them make the discoveries.

The best way to learn a story is to share it yourself. So ask them if they can think of anyone else in their life (spouse, kids, friends, etc.) who they think would be encouraged by the story as well. If they do (you'll be amazed!) it's helpful to review the story with them again or send them a text with a copy of it. Then ask them something like this, "Let me know how it goes with applying the story to your life this week and when you get to share it. If it goes well, I would be more than happy to share another one with you to pass on as well." And then follow up with them. Sometimes their interest will fizzle out, and that's ok. But you'll be surprised by how many people are moved by the story you shared with them and eager to share it with others.

Here's a story to put some flesh on what we've talked about the last few days:

My wife, Rachel, sat next to Francine for three hours at a kid's birthday party. The conversation started casual, but it was a long

DAY 11: MOVING FROM SPIRITUAL TO DISCOVERY CONVERSATIONS

party and the talk turned to dealing with the summer struggles of moms. Rachel came home bummed because she had never gotten around to turning the conversation to spiritual. But she kept praying for Francine, and a few days later Rachel worked up the nerve to text her, share that she'd been praying for her, and send her an encouraging Bible verse. Francine responded warmly, genuinely touched and said that the verse was exactly what she needed. A few days later Rachel sent her a full Bible story about Jesus calming the storm. Again Francine responded about how perfect that story was, and they exchanged different observations via post-bedtime texts. Rachel encouraged her to share it with her kids. And then she took the plunge and asked Francine if she would be interested in studying more Bible stories together. Francine was eager and asked if she could invite a neighbor mom, too. When the kids returned to school, they started meeting weekly, and at last count there were five moms involved.

Day Eleven Challenge

1. Think of stories from the Bible that could bring encouragement to a person if they . . .

    Are stressed and anxious: _____

    Are struggling with a broken relationship: _____

    Have a loved one that is sick..._____

2. Read Mark 4:35–41 twice and practice retelling the story in your own words. Then ask a friend who has some stress in their life (who doesn't?) if you can share a short story that you think would encourage them. If it goes well, apply what you learned from today.

3. Check out Appendix A for a list of more Bible stories that I like to use.

HABIT #3

MEETING WITH YOUR DISCIPLE

(DAYS 12 THROUGH 17)

Note: Hopefully you've caught that this whole process is considered "disciple making," but this is the stage where you begin to study God's Word together with someone previously far from God, which looks a lot more like our traditional understanding of "discipleship."

DAY 12

making it official

How did yesterday's challenge go? Did you share the Bible story with anyone? How did they respond? (If you didn't do it yet, go do it now!)

I met Rachel on our college cross country team, but I really began to be attracted to her while we served the homeless in Los Angeles. For Valentine's Day I colluded with her roommate so that Rachel woke up to a long-stem red rose on her desk and a simple note that read, "Will you be my valentine? Check appropriate box, yes or not no." She never really had a chance. That was our first DTR (Define the Relationship).

Jesus did the same sort of thing with each of his disciples when he approached them with very clear words: "Come follow me." Jesus could have just assumed his disciples were committed because they kept hanging around his ministry, but he chose to make the invitation clear to the ones he was most invested in. At some point we need to do the same when it comes to the people we disciple.

After you've shared multiple Bible stories with a person, and they have an undeniable interest in learning more about God, you will need to "make it official." If you stay in this phase of just sharing stories with a short informal discussion for too long, it

DAY 12: MAKING IT OFFICIAL

will likely stunt their growth from becoming a fully surrendered disciple. On the flip side, you also want to be careful not to move this process along too quickly. It may be obvious to you that they are an answer to your prayers in finding someone to disciple, but when we rush the process and push too hard, they can often fizzle out, like the seed on shallow, rocky soil. In my own experience I usually have the "make it official" conversation between three and ten Bible story meetings, depending on their consistency and leading from the Holy Spirit.

Here's how I do it: Set up an extended time to meet in person (assuming you live near each other) and share how you've really enjoyed studying Bible stories together. Then invite them into a more intentional journey of discovering God and what He has to say about life. It's important that you present a picture of what it would look like going forward, letting them experience what a typical time together would look like.

As a side note, we've included several great resources in the back of the book that you can use or further explore. One is the *Across the Table* discipleship material created specifically for this phase of disciple making (see Appendix B). Another simple template used all around the world is the Discovery Bible Study Method (Appendix C). Regardless of the material you use there are four *big picture* elements that you just can't miss, and we will be talking about these over the next few days: Friendship, Discovery, Obedience, and Celebration.

After experiencing the study together, ask if they are interested in meeting weekly to learn and obey together in a similar format. If they agree, decide on the details:

- When and where are we going to meet? (I've found that meeting in person is always better, but not always easier. I often meet with my disciples one week in person and the next on zoom or the phone.)

- How long are we making this commitment for? (The disciple-making material you're using will likely help guide this one.)

- Is there anyone else that you think should join us? (We will talk more about discipling groups in a few days.)

Bringing It All together

I met Sonya and Peter while they were washing their truck in their apartment complex parking lot. I was prayer walking and I simply asked if there was anything I could pray for them. If they could have one miracle happen in their lives, what would it be? Sonya openly shared about her past that included addictions and prison time. She had five kids, and her past had been especially difficult on her youngest daughter.

"Before I pray for you and your daughter, can I share with you a short story from the Bible that I think would encourage you?" I asked. I shared the story of the Prodigal Son, and by the end she was in tears. Over the next few weeks I shared several more stories with them that they were passing on to other family members and co-workers. After the fifth story, we sat in their apartment, and I walked them through a Discovery Bible Study. They excitedly accepted the invitation to keep meeting regularly. Through our times together over the following months, the Holy Spirit spoke to them and challenged them directly through God's

Word and, eventually, I got the privilege of baptizing Sonya.

Their story is a beautiful example of how hungry people often are for the hope Jesus offers, and how simple it can be to invite them into a discipling relationship.

Day Twelve Challenge

If there is someone in your life that makes sense to do this with, set up the meeting. If not, keep working on your prayer calendar and intentional conversations and ask a Christian friend (spouse, parent, sibling, child, etc.) to have a role play conversation with you where you can practice what you learned today.

DAY 13

don't you dare teach them

How did yesterday's conversation challenge go? Don't move forward 'til . . . (you know!)

I was a little bit terrified when I first volunteered to be my son's soccer coach. I had a hard enough time keeping one five-year-old's attention let alone adding nine more. I also hadn't played soccer since I was in the sixth grade and didn't know much more than yelling "kick the ball!" After an hour of watching YouTube videos and scribbling drills I didn't totally understand on a three-by-five card, I was pleasantly shocked to discover that the league provided experienced coaches at all the practices; all I had to do was follow their lead.

That's a lot like how disciple making is. It's easy to be intimidated the first time, but the good news is that our role is more of an assistant coach. Listen to what Jesus said in John 6:44, 45:

> *"No one can come to me unless the Father who sent me draws them, and I will raise them up at the last day. It is written in the Prophets: 'They will all be taught by God.' Everyone who has heard the Father and learned from him comes to me."*

DAY 13: DON'T YOU DARE TEACH THEM

According to Jesus, no one can come to him unless, what?

Unless the Father draws them. It's the Father's job to draw people to himself, not ours. The first time I learned that it was as if a huge weight fell off my shoulders. Their being drawn or being raised up to heaven at the end of their lives isn't dependent on how well I deliver a rehearsed presentation or if I know all the right answers to their questions. He's either drawing them or He's not.

According to the verses, what is God's other job?

It's his job to do the teaching. This is a game changer, too, because he's a way better teacher than I am!

Jesus also shares here about what the seeker's role is in coming to Him. Can you find it? It is triple emphasized.

Everyone who comes to Jesus needs to actively "be taught by God" and "hear him" and "learn from him." Anybody who has ever sat in a classroom knows that just because the teacher is teaching doesn't mean the students are being taught. There is a humility and attentiveness required by those listening. The Greek word for *heard* here means to "obey" or "put into practice." This is the same word Jesus often ended his parables with when he said, "he who has ears, let him hear." He didn't mean this teaching is for you if you have two physical ears. He was urging his followers to "hear" as in "to put [his words] into practice."

So Jesus's promise is that he will do the drawing and teaching, and if the seeker agrees to be taught by God and put it into practice, then they will come to Jesus. Every time.

Did you notice who is not mentioned in these verses?

Us!

What, then, is our role in people coming to Jesus? It's a lot less than you might think. We're simply called to help others get into environments where they can be taught by God (Discovery) and then help them put their learning into practice (Accountability).

Therefore, the discipleship material you use *must* be discovery based. Don't you dare try to teach them. While God certainly uses people with teaching or preaching gifts, we must set up God as their primary teacher. Here are two main ways we can do this.

Discovery through God's Word

A primary part of your time together is simply reading God's Word and allowing them to discover truths from it directly. Don't turn these Bible studies into opportunities for you to sermonize. If there are truths you want them to grasp, be patient and get them there by asking good questions. The more open-ended and the less leading the questions are the better. The Discovery Bible Study method simply uses three general questions that can be used with any passage: What does it teach you about God? What does it teach you about people? What does it teach you about the life God is calling you to live? So many times I come into a meeting with what I think are good insights on a passage, and these new believers blow me away with something I had never thought of before.

Discovery through God's Spirit

You must create space where they learn to be quiet before God and to identify his promptings and still small voice. The

DAY 13: DON'T YOU DARE TEACH THEM

Across the Table resources use an ancient prayer experience called Lectio Divina where we ask God's Spirit to bring to life God's Word in the here and now. The goal is for your disciple to naturally start saying things like, "God is teaching me that . . ." or "I think God's Spirit is leading me toward . . ." See Exhibit B for a sample spread from an *Across the Table* journal or visit churchleaders.com/discipleship for more information.

A message *discovered* is infinitely more powerful than a message *delivered*. It also makes our job as disciple makers a lot easier.

It was life changing for my new-believer friend Oscar to realize that he didn't need to know all the theological answers or spend hours prepping a lesson to lead his family and friends in a Bible study. When I showed him how to simply create a space where they could learn from God by themselves, he dove head-first into disciple making. He had grown up in a Catholic background where it felt like the Bible could only be understood by the trained professionals. An infectious joy came from him learning, not just *about* God, but *from* God personally.

Day Thirteen Challenge

Think of someone in your life who is stressed and ask if you can share with them a short story that you think would encourage them. (You pick the story today.) Ask them what they learn about Jesus from this story and how it could apply to their life.

DAY 14

celebrating stories and steps of faith

How did yesterday's challenge go? Look it over before moving on today.

On the last day of each week of our journey I share a story of one of my friends on their own journey of becoming a multiplying disciple maker. Let me introduce you to Jose:

I was born and raised in New York, but being a Marine for the past 20 years, I've traveled a lot and currently live in Southern California. I've always had incredibly high standards and expectations for myself and my Marines. While I am certainly not soft nor gentle with them, I have always done my best to provide them with grace, reminding myself that we all falter and make mistakes because no one is perfect. I also try to keep my anger in check and prevent myself from using foul language—character traits which are extremely rare in Marine culture. I had even once offered to lead a Bible study to any of my Marines, but none had taken me up on it. These were my ways of trying to be a Jesus follower at work, but I was discouraged by my lack of fruit.

I was introduced to this Disciple Making training, and at first, I was skeptical. I knew how spiritually closed everyone around me was, so what good would these simple steps and tools be? But with nothing to lose, I started following the steps and being more intentional in my conversations with my Marines and other friends.

One day an old friend with no spiritual beliefs responded to my prayer calendar text with a vague request. I reluctantly texted a prayer back to him, trying to follow the "rules." His response blew me away. He quickly wrote back that he had had plenty of people tell him they were praying for him over the years, but he never knew what that meant. But reading the words of my prayer (which, trust me, were nothing spectacular!) impacted him and he started opening up with me spiritually. This disciple making thing was working!

Sometimes progress still feels slow, but at least I'm moving in the right direction.

Chris was attached to my section but initially I had little interaction with him because there were multiple levels of leadership between us. I became more hands-on after I was alerted by a peer of his that he had posted a suicidal message on his social media. Chris received medical and psychiatric assistance, and after a few months he appeared to have taken a turn for the better. Then he had a second suicidal situation and continued to struggle. Eventually he was removed from our work section for his safety.

After about six months he once again returned to our work section, and this time he immediately approached me. He remembered me inviting Marines to church and offering to do

Bible studies with them. Chris shared that while he knew he needed help back when I'd made the offer, he just wasn't ready to step forward. This time was different, and he knew he needed to accept everyone that was willing to help, including God.

We started meeting regularly and have continued meeting even since my retirement. During our time together we start by simply catching up on the previous week. We share any praises or situations that we recognize as blessings. Then we discuss any struggles that we may be facing and pray for each other. We decided to start by studying simple stories about Jesus. We read the story twice and then take turns retelling it in our own words, so we feel like we've got a good handle on it. Then we simply answer a few questions about what the story teaches us about God and ourselves and how we could apply it to our lives. Finally, we discuss who we could share the story with. It's been cool hearing how Chris shares whatever story we study that week with his roommate.

Chris has also gotten in the habit of sharing that week's passage with several of his friends who also suffer with depression and suicidal ideations. His hope is that these lessons that are helping him will do the same for them.

For me, this whole experience has grown me so much in my faith. It's powerful to see life change happen in someone else. Discipling someone has made me much more comfortable discussing my beliefs with others and going beyond surface level in conversations. Whereas, before, I would just try to drop Christian jargon in conversation like "God's good" or "I'm so blessed," now I feel more confident in offering to pray for someone or sharing a Bible story that relates to their struggle, and it's amazing how many more people are open!

Lastly, it's been an enormous and unexpected blessing to see how growing as a disciple maker has impacted my kids. On her own volition, our ten-year-old daughter invited her sister and a bunch of their friends to start a weekly Discovery Bible Study (DBS). In their case DBS stands for the three things they bring every week: doll, Bible, and a snack.

Day Fourteen Challenge

Look over your "I will" statements from this past week. How did they go? Were you obedient? Are you ready for Week 3 or do you have some unfinished steps to take?

DAY 15

obedience based disciple making

Are you ready to start a new week of challenges?

The most helpful thing about premarital counseling for Rachel and me was learning about our love languages. We are complete opposites, and as a naïve 24-year-old, I was aghast when I scored a big, fat zero in identifying hers. I have had many years of practicing *acts of service* since then!

I know Jesus predates the *Love Languages* book by two thousand years, but he sure seems to have his own love language. Can you guess what it is? Read through John 14 and 15 if you want to score better than I did with Rachel.

More than just "acts of service," Jesus makes it clear that he feels loved through our obedience. Yet discipleship nowadays tends to lean so much more toward knowledge acquisition. Absolutely, there are core truths that young disciples need to learn, but knowing the truth and living it out are not the same thing. And which one makes Jesus feel more loved? A seasoned Christian who knows a lot about the original Greek and fifteen arguments for dispensationalism . . . but hasn't practically applied a verse from their daily Bible reading in years? Or, a brand-new believer who doesn't even know all the normal Sunday school stories, but is obeying God's Word each day after reading it?

In our Christian culture today we are often educated far beyond our levels of obedience. So as you disciple others it is imperative that you cultivate a culture from day one that God's Word is meant to be obeyed.

Here are a couple of ways to build a culture of obedience:

Always Have an Application Step

Many disciple makers call this an "I will" statement. Don't leave without having each person say, "Because of today's passage, I will . . . [forgive a friend, start reading the Bible on my own, use a respectful voice with my parents, confess a lie, etc.]" It's important that the application is specific. Vague is the enemy to spiritual growth. Instead of sharing that you're going to love more this week (number one vague application), share that you're going to show love to your co-worker by taking them to lunch this week. "I will" statements don't have to be huge. You can get a lot further with consistent small steps than with failed big steps.

Never Skip the Accountability Step

We improve on what we inspect. Coming up with a way to obey that day's passage is only helpful if you ask each other how it went the next time you meet.

Now, accountability sometimes has a negative stigma because people have experienced it in one of two extremes. Guilt-based Accountability is where we make the person feel bad because they didn't follow through on an obedience step. Guilt is a tool of the Enemy, not God, so we need to avoid pressuring people with it. But Excessive-Grace Accountability is the opposite problem. In seeking not to offend, we create a culture where it doesn't really matter if you obey or not, which renders accountability useless.

Instead we must seek to celebrate obedience and learn from our experiences. If a person's obedience step was to read the Bible daily and they were only successful one day, then say something like, "Is this still a habit you want to live out? What could you do differently to make this week go better? What did you learn from the one day that you were successful?" Then encourage them to make this their obedience step again instead of coming up with a new one. The following week when they improve, celebrate that God is working powerfully in them.

Or, if they realize that their obedience step just wasn't doable for whatever reason, help them process their next one into something more manageable.

Around the world where disciple making is exploding, a common phrase is, "Learn one thing. Do one thing." Why would we ever move on to something new before we start obeying what we already learned?

Be a Super-Model

If you're a parent you've learned that your kids don't do what you tell them to do, they do what you do. If you don't lead by example with your "I will" statements, that's the lesson the person you are discipling will learn from you.

I introduced you earlier to Peter and Sonya. A couple weeks into meeting together studying stories about Jesus, they shared that they had an additional question they wanted my help with.

"What does God think about sex outside of marriage?"

I knew the power of discovery, so I directed them to a few passages that clearly spoke about sex being a gift from God reserved for married relationships.

"That's what we thought."

They had been living together for more than five years without thought, but Jesus was already transforming them. A few days later they reached out to me to ask another question.

"Would you marry us as soon as possible? We want to obey God in everything we do."

A few weeks later their adult children and grandchildren showed up to our backyard for a small ceremony. I shared the Prodigal Son story just as I had when I first met their parents. They turned to their kids and said, "From now on we are seeking to live life God's way." Their obedience was more impactful to their family than anything they could have said.

Day Fifteen Challenge

What's an area in your life that you'd honestly not want someone to emulate? (Language, weak prayer life, purity . . . ?) What's a small, specific step you could take to grow in this area? Call a Christian friend and ask if they will keep you accountable.

DAY 16

discipling to conversion and baptizing new believers

How did yesterday's challenge go? What baby step have you taken?

DAY 16: DISCIPLING TO CONVERSION AND BAPTIZING NEW BELIEVERS

During my fifteen years as a youth pastor, perhaps my most effective evangelistic tool was Costco. At least once a week I would pick up a student after school and drive to the best deal in town. I'd get to know their story as we strolled the aisles looking for free samples. Afterwards I would treat us to a hotdog and a coke for $3.23 total. (I know, big spender!) After praying for the food I'd almost always transition the conversation into spiritual things to learn about their faith background. It was natural for me to then share what I believed, which almost always entailed drawing a picture of a bridge on a Costco napkin and giving the student an opportunity to pray and receive Christ as their Lord and Savior.

I still love our local Costco, but as I reflect on many of those prayers, I know they were not all salvation moments. Some students never took any additional faith steps—as hard as I tried to help them—and just continued with their previous way of living life before praying "the prayer." And this isn't just a teenager issue. Over the years I've witnessed thousands of adults raise their hand in an Easter service, make no life changes, and disappear until their next visit on Christmas Eve. Without getting too tangled in the theological implications of "eternal security," let's look at this from another angle.

Jesus's encounter with Zacchaeus is one of my favorite stories in the Gospels, but it's a lot different than my Costco trips. Jesus was hanging in the little, tax-collector's home when the host announces that he was going to give most of his money away to the poor and those he'd cheated in the past. Jesus responds, "Today salvation has come to this house." Wait a minute. There is no indication that Zacchaeus prayed any sort of salvation prayer, or even that he comprehended Jesus's role as Messiah. Yet Jesus declares him (and his home?) saved. Is that allowed?

In his book *Spent Matches*, **Roy Moran** describes the perilous shift in our concept of salvation, saying, "Instead of figuring out how to disciple—teaching to identify with Jesus and to obey Him—we drifted toward converting people to a set of propositions and then attempting to get them to understand that Jesus wants to be more than a Savior." When we convince people that they only need to say a few words to be saved, their pursuit of ongoing discipleship can be noncommittal. And we're guilty of a bait and switch. But if we teach them from the beginning to listen to and obey God, then their conversion and baptism are simply an important and exciting step in that discipling process. An ongoing, disciple-making relationship for the new believer isn't just more likely, it's also natural because it already exists and it's all they've experienced.

Please hear me on this, I'm not calling into question every spontaneous salvation presentation, nor am I saying that there is any other way to a relationship with Jesus than by grace through faith. But that obedient relationship with Jesus requires more than a prayer.

Here are three helpful mindsets to have as a disciple maker:

Seek Disciple-Making Relationships over Salvation Prayers

This is especially imperative in our post-Christian culture, where people need to learn what it means to be a Jesus follower. As we've talked about all last week, find those interested in spiritual conversation and invite them into hearing and obeying

DAY 16: DISCIPLING TO CONVERSION AND BAPTIZING NEW BELIEVERS

God through His Word and Spirit. It's a longer process but worth the wait.

Let Your Disciple Discover Salvation

Let me illustrate. Recently I was meeting with a couple that had not yet received Jesus but were enjoying studying Bible stories with me each week. We were studying the story in Mark 2 where Jesus heals the paralyzed man lowered into the room. They made the observation that having your sins forgiven seemed to be really important to Jesus. Then the wife blurted out, "Wouldn't it be an amazing feeling to *know* your sins were forgiven?" In *that* moment I seized the opportunity and shared how Jesus's death made that possible, and they gladly received Christ as their Lord and Savior.

Baptize as Soon as Possible

In every case except one in the New Testament, people got baptized ON THE SAME DAY they decided to follow Jesus. My friend leads a ministry called Total Fit that has used fitness to plant thousands of churches and groups all over the world. They did an in-depth study and found that when someone gets baptized very soon after their conversion only 12 percent of the new believers go back to their old life. However, when someone delays their baptism for special classes to be prepared, the number jumps to 48 percent returning to their old way of life.

When I first heard that stat I thought he said it backwards. Doesn't it make sense to take them through a new-believer class first or to wait until they feel ready? But Jesus is looking for followers who obey, and baptism is an amazing opportunity right out of the gate to say, "Even if I don't totally understand everything, I'm surrendered to Christ now and will do what he says."

I usually take a new believer through several passages about baptism (see Appendix D) and let them discover for themselves what their first step as a follower of Christ should be and how long they should wait. Their baptism could happen at church on a Sunday, but it could also happen on a Thursday night in a backyard with friends and family. I know different denominations view this differently, but as a Jesus follower you're not only allowed to baptize people (or be a key part of their baptism), but you're also commanded to—wherever and however you believe is proper.

Day Sixteen Challenge

Are there any Christians in your life that you know have not been baptized? Ask if you can meet with them to share a story. Discuss Acts 8:26–40 and just ask what they learn from the story in terms of baptism and what application they should take. If you can't think of anyone, study the passage with any friend or family member as practice.

DAY 17

disciple is spelled f-r-i-e-n-d

How did yesterday's challenge go? How did your friend respond to the passage about baptism? What observations did you make about what the passage teaches?

Jesus saved you primarily for a mission to accomplish.

That sounds really spiritual, doesn't it? Find out what God has put you on the planet to do for him, and then do it.

While that's not totally wrong, it's also not totally accurate. Why *did* Jesus save us? Look at Mark 3:13, 14:

> *Jesus went up on a mountainside and called to him those he wanted, and they came to him. He appointed twelve* **that they might be with him** *and that he might send them out to preach.*

Jesus's primary desire in calling his disciples was "that they might be with him." More than anything that Jesus wants *from* us, he wants an intimate relationship *with* us. Even the next phrase—"that he might send them out to preach"—was the result of what He would do as they spent time together.

He makes their relationship crazy clear, again, on his last night with them . . .

> *Greater love has no one than this: to lay down one's life for one's friends. You are my friends if you do what I command.*

John 15:13, 14

Paul lived out this relational ministry as well. Listen to his letter to the Thessalonians:

> *Just as a nursing mother cares for her children, so we cared for you. Because we loved you so*

DAY 17: DISCIPLE IS SPELLED F-R-I-E-N-D

*much, we were delighted to share with you not only the gospel of God but **our very lives as well.***

2 Thessalonians 2:7, 8

If this is how Jesus and Paul saw the people they poured into, then it's important we do the same. We can't treat our lives like a TV dinner and compartmentalize it all. When God blesses us with someone to disciple we can't just squeeze them into a nice, sixty-minute meeting each week. We must invite them into our lives—our home, our family, our schedule. Long before they begin to understand the love of Christ through studying the Bible together, they should feel the love of Christ just by being a part of our lives.

This may sound all nice, but it will stretch you.

A friend of ours now has a single mom living with her. Another friend has spent late nights supporting a struggling disciple over the phone. This will require time, energy, and resources. But it is so worth it!

Rachel and I were prayer walking with our three young kids in a nearby neighborhood, with the hope of starting conversations and praying for people on the spot. Now, normally when I see someone exercising, I don't try to interrupt, but in this case I sensed the Holy Spirit tell me to stop the Hispanic woman power walking toward us.

"Excuse me. Can I ask you a quick question?"

"Lo siento, no hablo inglés." (We were off to a no bueno beginning.)

Yet through our limited Spanish and her limited English, she eagerly shared a transparent prayer request for her husband to get work as a painter. It had been several months since his last job, and their finances were critically low. I shared a Bible story with her (I think she mostly understood) and we prayed . . . and then she said something we did not see coming.

"Pueden venir a mi casa esta tarde para conocer a mi familia?" (Will you come to my house this afternoon to meet my whole family?)

I knew this Spanish word perfectly. "Sí."

That afternoon we had a great time with her family (including two sons fluent in English). Two days later she called my wife to share excitedly that they had received two painting jobs and they were all praising God! Since then our very different families have become good friends. We've eaten in each other's homes, cheered for each other's kids at soccer games, helped them start a Discovery Bible Study with other friends and family, and now several family members have been baptized.

Now, this might sound like I'm simply describing Friendship Evangelism, which is a really good thing. But I want to make an important distinction that will hopefully be a game changer for you.

In Friendship Evangelism, the goal is to befriend someone so that over time you can earn the right share Jesus with them one day. While this can be effective, you've likely had disappointing experiences where either you never got around to sharing, or after investing lots of time in a friendship, you find that they really have no interest in spiritual things. In our crazy busy world it's easy to surround ourselves with so many relationships that there is too little time to discover or invest in those who are interested in spiritual things.

But, in Disciple Making, you'll notice this slight but significant change in focus: rather than investing lots of time earning the right to share your faith, be spiritually intentional in your conversations from the beginning in order to discern their spiritual interest up front. Remember, we don't need to convince people to learn about spiritual things; we simply discover people who are already convinced. Then we choose to pursue a deeper friendship with those people.

Day Seventeen Challenge

Be quiet before the Lord for a few minutes and ask him what you should specifically do today based on what you just read.

Write down what he says:

_____

_____

_____

_____

Now obey.

HABIT #4

MULTIPLYING DISCIPLES

(DAYS 18 THROUGH 21)

DAY 18

inviting the whole oikos

What did God whisper to you yesterday? Did you do it?

In Acts 16, Paul and Silas plant a church in the city of Philippi that never should have made it. Not by modern church planting strategy standards at least. They only stayed in the Roman-run city for probably a week, and just as they were gaining traction they were severely beaten, imprisoned, and then kicked out of town. They left behind two newly converted Christian families from very different backgrounds who didn't know each other. This was the core team. Yet, years later Paul writes a letter to this church which is clearly thriving.

How did this happen?

Paul and Silas tapped into the power of oikos, and they left us a valuable example to follow with their brand-new disciples. Let's observe . . .

First, they meet a woman named Lydia at a prayer gathering outside the city.

> *When she **and the members of her household** were baptized, she invited us to her home. "If you consider me a believer in the Lord," she*

> said, *"come and stay at my house."* And she
> persuaded us.

Acts 16:15

A few days later while Paul and Silas sing worship songs in prison, God brings an earthquake, and the jailer becomes another very unexpected member of the team. Paul tells him,

> *"Believe in the Lord Jesus, and you will be saved—you and **your household.**" Then they spoke the word of the Lord to him and to all the **others in his house**. At that hour of the night the jailer took them and washed their wounds; then immediately he and **all his household** were baptized. The jailer brought them into his house and set a meal before them; he was filled with joy because he had come to believe in God—he and **his whole household.***

Acts 16:31–34

What do you notice about both conversions? (Besides, of course, their immediate baptism, as we've already discussed.) Notice that Paul included their "household" in the conversion and baptism. The Greek word used here—and all throughout the New Testament—is *oikos*, which, as we have learned before, means more than just family, but also includes your closest relational networks.

Paul and Silas's strategy in Philippi is not unique in this approach. Out of the thirty-three conversions in the book of Acts, thirty of

DAY 18: INVITING THE WHOLE OIKOS

them occur in oikoses—groups—who collectively decide to put their hope in Christ. And this is still happening today in most parts of the world where the gospel is exploding.

In contrast, the modern Western church primarily uses an individual evangelism model. It makes sense that because our society is so individualistically focused we would naturally emphasize people making a personal commitment to follow Christ. This is how most of us probably decided to follow Christ, and so we pass on what we've personally experienced.

But take a moment to consider natural group and family dynamics. What is the impact if a 16-year-old daughter goes to youth group with a friend and decides to give her life to Christ? Maybe—hopefully—her unbelieving family sees the difference in her life and she leads them all to find God. But more often than not her decision leads to being divided in how she thinks and spends her time, trying to balance her family with her new church "family." It leads to her family being concerned that she's trapped in a cult or feeling negative toward the changes they see in her. And this growing tension often leads to either the girl walking away from her new faith or else the family being turned off to the church that changed her. (I've witnessed both tragic scenarios far too often!)

But imagine if this same 16-year-old were discipled by a friend in the way we are learning about, so that she went home after each meeting and shared what she was learning with her family. And instead of spending all her time in a new church family, she intentionally engaged them in her spiritual discovery, so that her parents and siblings all decided to follow Christ together at relatively the same time. What would likely result from this scenario? You'd likely find that this family experiences unity in pursuing Jesus together, encouragement to help each other grow in their new faith, and a new group identity in who "we" are now in Christ.

Of course it doesn't always happen this way, but can we agree that it's better when oikos groups decide to follow Christ together?

In traditional church settings there will be unsaved seekers and baby Christians who need to be discipled. So be on the lookout for people who God wants you to develop a disciple-making relationship with and help them reach their families and friends.

But as disciple makers, we need to bring Jesus to those farthest from church as well. In the city where I live, surveys report that a majority of people indicate that they will never come to a Christian church no matter what. Things could happen in their life where that changes, but for many, it won't. Often their opposition comes from growing up in a different faith background (in the same way that I don't envision myself ever regularly attending a mosque), or they are carrying hurts from the church. Yet this aversion to church does not equate to an aversion to Jesus. In fact, I've found that sometimes these are the most spiritually open people when I meet them where they're at.

If you are discipling someone who has an aversion to church (or their family/friends/oikos are opposed), that's ok. The next step is simply to ask your person who they know that might want to discover more about God with them.

Then help them create a space where their whole family/friends/co-workers/teammates group can discover truth about God together. Help them decide on a time and location. Show them the simplicity of the materials you've been using. Transition your discipling meetings to help them prepare for their group. And resist the urge to invite them to all meet with you. Remember, you're not a part of their oikos and will hinder them from coming, or hold back their growth more than you will help it.

This all may sound a little idealistic and impossible; but isn't that how it happened in Philippi? Paul and Silas invested in Lydia and the jailer, who then took what they learned to help their families grow as well. Obviously their households spread the message to others, because amid trials a healthy church grew. In their case, Paul and Silas had to flee town, but fortunately we get to meet with our disciples regularly as they help bring along their whole oikos. What excuse do we have?

Day Eighteen Challenge

Share what you learned today with one friend who has family members or friends who have been resistant to attending church.

DAY 19

disciples that make disciples
that make disciples

Did you share what you learned with a friend yesterday? How did they respond?

_____
_____
_____
_____
_____
_____
_____
_____
_____
_____

DAY 19: DISCIPLES THAT MAKE DISCIPLES THAT MAKE DISCIPLES

I shared in the introduction about the parable of the four soils. Over the past three weeks you have been developing habits which will help you live your life in the good soil that will reproduce. A fruitful life is what Jesus desires, but the true power of this parable is found in the second generation. What happens when the thirty, sixty, or one hundred people you pour into during your lifetime all make thirty, sixty, or one hundred disciples of their own? Albert Einstein said that compound interest is the eighth great wonder of the world. Compound fruitfulness was Jesus's plan to reach it.

Consider Jesus's words to his disciples in Matthew 9:37, 38:

> *The harvest is plentiful but the workers are few. Ask the Lord of the harvest, therefore, to send out workers into his harvest field.*

Have you ever struggled with Jesus's words here, wondering just where this plentiful harvest is? I know I've sometimes complained that it must have dried up in the past two thousand years. But notice what Jesus describes as the problem: "the workers are few." And Jesus's solution? He doesn't tell his disciples to pray for more harvest but rather to pray for more workers—more disciple makers.

Then check out what Jesus does next! In the first verses of chapter 10, Jesus calls his twelve disciples by name and then sends them out on their first mission trip. Talk about the ultimate bait and switch! Jesus tells them to pray for more workers . . . and then immediately turns to them and basically says, "Great! I'm going to make you the answer to your own prayer."

A few chapters later Jesus sends them out again, and now there are seventy-two workers. I may struggle with my kids' math homework, but even I can figure this out. 12 x 6 = 72. This is multiplication at work!

Jesus wants to use you to raise up more disciple makers as well. The harvest *is* still there, and the lack of workers is still preventing bringing it in.

I love introducing people to the Great Commission as we talk about their baptism. At this point their discovery that our relationship has been propelled by my obedience to Jesus' final words is meaningful. At their baptism, then, I ask the normal questions about if they've accepted Jesus as their Savior and if it is their intention to follow Christ with their life. But now I add, "And is it your desire to make disciples and baptize others?" It's huge for them to understand that they are now a part of something much bigger than just a "personal" relationship between them and God.

And when it "clicks," it's awesome.

Juan had grown up with no spiritual background. Using the habits we've learned in this book, I started sharing stories with him from the Bible and saw Juan move from an atheist to a Jesus follower. After his baptism our family was invited to his son's 2-year-old birthday party. We were the only non-family members. Juan introduced me to his cousin Adrian. He shared how we had first met when I had shared a Bible story with him.

"That must have been some story. Can I hear it?" Adrian asked.

DAY 19: DISCIPLES THAT MAKE DISCIPLES THAT MAKE DISCIPLES

Without skipping a beat, Juan broke into his paraphrased version of the ten lepers story found in Luke 17. He led the three of us in a discovery discussion about the passage and then asked Adrian to share the story with the rest of his family and let him know how it went. It took everything inside of me not to explode in celebration. Juan was living this out!

As I was leaving later, Adrian tracked me down and gave me a hug. He shared that he was so excited to start meeting with his cousin to learn how he could be a spiritual leader to his family.

Click.

My friend Ricardo (who I baptized several months ago) called me last week to tell me that a guy he had baptized went on to baptize a friend who went on to baptize another one of their friends. He said it so nonchalantly, as if four generations of baptisms within a few months period was a normal thing.

Maybe it's supposed to be.

As we near the end of this twenty-one day, disciple-making challenge, take a minute to envision going through this book again with a disciple who you've baptized, and then watching them baptize someone else. It's not as far out there as it was three weeks ago. You can see it happening now, can't you? That is evidence that God is growing your faith muscles.

Day Nineteen Challenge

Look back to Day 5 when you used the FRANCE sheet to write out names. Pray over each of them that they would not only become disciples but also become disciple makers.

DAY 20

when it doesn't go the way you planned

Warning: I'm going to share my favorite and most frustrating disciple making story thus far.

I was prayer walking with a friend in a nearby apartment complex when I saw a Hispanic man slightly older than me painting a building. He was obviously busy, and I made an unfair assumption that he didn't speak English, so I started to walk by. But I suddenly got a strong sense that I was supposed to talk to him, so I stopped and "bothered" him anyway. I shared that we were praying over the complex and wanted to see if there was any way we could pray for him.

Surprisingly he said yes and shared in perfect English about his uncle living in El Paso who had recently been admitted to the hospital—and his family was told not to expect him to return home. I shared the story about Jesus calming the sea with my new friend named Rafael, and he agreed to pass it on to his adult kids and uncle. We exchanged numbers, and the following week he texted me asking if I'd meet him again at the complex where he was working so that I could share another Bible story! I was surprised again, but of course I eagerly met him on his lunch break.

Over the next few weeks Rafael started sharing the Bible stories with his whole family, who were all equally interested in spiritual things. He shared the stories with his co-workers, and THEY began passing them on to their families at home. Rafael was even having spiritual conversations with residents of the apartments that he was painting.

And I started seeing God do stuff that I thought He only did in other countries. I prayed for his hospitalized uncle on the phone, and a few days later Rafael told me that he was released from the hospital with the doctors having no explanation for his sudden healing. One visit, Rafael hurried me over to meet a woman and her daughter in their apartment. They asked me to pray for the mother's feet, which were in great pain for many years. The woman slipped off her sandals and they expected me to touch her feet . . . which I reluctantly did while I prayed the worst, most faithless prayer ever (as I tried not to think about what I was touching). Suddenly the mother jumped up and started dancing and praising God that her feet were healed. Her daughter was shocked and confirmed that she hadn't seen her nearly crippled mother move like that in years!

About two months into our meetings, Rafael and I were studying Genesis 1 where God said, "Let us make man in our image." My friend made the deep observation that if all people are made in God's image, then all humans are inherently valuable to God. And then, out of nowhere, Rafael burst into tears. Right there in the middle of the apartment complex.

"Jim, I need to share something with you that I was at first ashamed of, but I now realize will actually bring God glory." I

DAY 20: WHEN IT DOESN'T GO THE WAY YOU PLANNED

leaned in. "A few months back I was dealing with some heavy depression coming from addiction issues. I had decided to take my own life and had even driven over to a specific railroad crossing several times where I believed I could make a suicide look like an accident to protect my family. I'd set the date for that Friday . . . when out of nowhere two strangers approached me on Wednesday asking if they could pray for me. They shared a Bible story that brought me peace and when they left, I whispered, 'God, if you exist, was that from you?' I heard an audible 'yes' and that I should do whatever this guy Jim says to do."

At this point there were tears in both of our eyes. Rafael looked at me and said, "Jim, Jesus saved my life through you. That's why I'm willing to do whatever He asks."

Amazing story, right? Almost like it's straight out of the book of Acts. But here's the part I wish I could leave out. About a month later Rafael changed job sites and stopped returning my texts and phone calls. I even tracked him down to his next worksite, but every time I've stopped by I've always just missed him, and he hasn't responded to any of the notes I've left with his co-workers. It's been about a year since we last spoke. What's up with that, God?

2 Timothy 2:2 is a famous disciple-making verse about passing what we've learned on to trustworthy people who will pass it on to others. Very inspiring. But perhaps verse 3 is even more important:

> *Join with me in suffering, like a good soldier of Christ Jesus.*

Paul made it clear to his young disciple that disciple-making is difficult. It comes with the highest highs but also sometimes the lowest lows. I can't think of a God-follower in the Bible that didn't suffer in their following God. We shouldn't expect anything different. Knowing this enables us to be prepared and have two necessary tools in place.

Stubborn Perseverance

We don't live the life of a disciple maker because it's easy but because our Savior commanded and empowered us to. On the frustrating days, I cling to Galatians 6:9:

> *Let us not become weary in doing good, for at the proper time we will reap a harvest if we do not give up.*

Community with Disciple Makers

Jesus sent out the disciples in twos because what he was calling them to would require side-by-side encouragement, accountability, and prayer. Two thousand years later it's still the same. Those who seek to live out the habits of a disciple maker alone usually end up quitting. You must regularly surround yourself with a few others who want to take the Great Commission as seriously as you do. From experience, I'd suggest you don't try to add this component on to an existing small group, but instead start a new one with people who also truly want to make growing as disciple makers a priority. That means weekly checking in for prayer, encouragement, and accountability.

DAY 20: WHEN IT DOESN'T GO THE WAY YOU PLANNED

Looking back, I don't regret one minute I spent with my friend Rafael, and I look forward to the day I finally get a text back from him. Or else a really good explanation when I see him in heaven.

Day Twenty Challenge

You've probably already experienced some discouragement over the past twenty days. Tell God how you honestly feel, but then make a fresh surrender to him to seek to make disciples no matter what.

DAY 21

celebrating stories and steps of faith

For our last day together I'm excited to introduce you to my friend Frank. Here is his disciple-making story:

I was born into a pastor's home so my early life seemed to pretty much revolve around church. My purpose and calling as a believer came into much clearer focus when I attended a Christian college and was introduced to people my age, especially young men, who were truly focused on living for Jesus. Following graduation and a summer mission trip, I joined a church that invited me into pastoral ministry, and for more than thirty-five years, I have continued that ministry in some form.

From my ministry experience, disciple making has been much more of a means to an end in order to have a strong church rather than a desire to have a church that is obedient to the Great Commission. While I would have always said disciple making was important, it honestly was not as much of a priority on a weekly basis as ministering to the needs of our church's own members.

A few years back I went through a simple training called Disciple Making Movements. It really helped me to reset priorities based on what the Bible says. Disciple making became a non-negotiable call to obedience by God that very much impacted my weekly rhythms and routines. These new rhythms have connected me with other disciple makers who uplift, encourage, and hold me accountable. And the commitment of having a weekly next-step statement that I report back to my team has kept me on track better than any other tool I have encountered.

And God has been opening my eyes to the harvest.

Once, while out prayer walking with a disciple-making partner, we came upon a couple who didn't have a lot of resources. They asked that we pray for God's provision for them. I shared the Bible story of Jesus telling Peter to go fishing then look in the fish for a coin to pay the temple tax with. We talked about all the different ways that God can provide for us, and they were intrigued by the story. I asked if there was a way we could stay in contact, and they said that they didn't have email or cellphones. So I invited them to the church that I pastor, which was only about ten minutes away.

In all honesty I assumed that I would never see them again. But three months later they showed up on a Sunday morning. They were blessed by the service and said that they would come again. After a few weeks I asked them if they had ever committed their lives to Jesus and been baptized. They had lots of questions but were ultimately baptized a few weeks later on Easter.

We began meeting weekly for a ten-week Bible study, just looking at stories of people encountering Jesus. We are still meeting. Each week we read and discuss a Bible story and look for ways to apply it to our lives. The couple are caretakers for the man's parents, who are Mormons, but each week they take the Bible story home and share it with his father and mother. These are people I would have never met, let alone baptized and discipled, if I didn't change how I prioritized my time as a pastor.

As someone who has been following Jesus for many years now, I have never experienced as much satisfaction as a believer than I feel now, simply because I'm seeking to make disciples by spending time among the lost. I've been married to my wife, Donna, for more than thirty-

DAY 21: CELEBRATING STORIES AND STEPS OF FAITH

seven years, and we have been in ministry together for almost all that time. Since I started being more intentional about making disciples, she has told me repeatedly that she has never seen me more alive with the Holy Spirit and with purpose for my life at any other time during our marriage. The simple beauty of obedience is a most powerful thing.

Day Twenty-One Challenge

Set a time within the next week to go on a personal prayer retreat where you spend at least an hour going through the prayer retreat template (Appendix E).

First, give this priority by making an appointment for it. Day/Time: _____

Then, actually go on the prayer retreat! I know I can't ask you about it tomorrow, but believe me, you'll be so glad you made this a priority.

CLOSING WORDS

what do i do now?

And the journey continues...

I am so glad that you made it through the last twenty-one days. (Whether that was an actual three weeks, or it took longer!) Way to go in finishing what you started! I hope that you've heard through these pages that despite the difficulty, there is incredible joy in practically living the life of a disciple maker.

You might be wondering now, what's next?

Well, let me share how I got from standing in my backyard in the middle of the night to living out all that I just shared over the past three weeks? It's not been easy, and I've had a lot of help.

After God's middle-of-the-night challenge I started reading everything I could get my hands on about disciple making. A few months in this led me to discover what God was doing around the world through Disciple-Making Movements. I had no idea that there were hundreds (now thousands) of places around the globe where the gospel was exploding through cities, nations, and continents. The average size of these movements was more than sixty thousand baptisms, and the churches looked quite a bit different than the ones I had been a part of or planted.

In that time, Gallup came out with a stat that rocked me. The church in North America had shrunk by 23 percent from 1999 to 2019. (This is pre-COVID.) This statistic was especially challenging to me because I started full-time ministry in 1999. So, on my watch (not that anyone has put me in charge of anything), nearly 1 out of 4 people had left the "Big C" Church. I am a HUGE fan and advocate of any church desiring to lower the percentage of lostness in their city, but this statistic paired with what was happening around the world started me asking, "Could there be another way?"

After about a year of searching I went through a simple Disciple-Making Movement training with a new friend named Chris Galanos who was a few years ahead of me on the same journey. I joined about fifty others to go through this training that is used all over the world—and it was like I could hear the whisper of God through all of it saying, "Jim, this is what I wanted you to find."

At one point we were reading Matthew 9:38 where Jesus says, "The harvest is plentiful but the workers are few." I'd read that verse a thousand times before but never made the obvious connection that Matthew 10 was a detailed description of what a worker looks like. I was deeply convicted that my life did not look at all like what Jesus sent the Twelve out to do, but not surprisingly, where these new movements were spreading, that's exactly what Jesus followers were doing. As a result, the last several years have been course correcting my schedule and priorities to be a worker in my local harvest field and to raise up many others.

I wholeheartedly believe that if you apply what we've studied together the past three weeks, you will see God move in your life in some exciting ways. If the thought of this excites you and makes you want more, I want to offer you the same invitation my friend Chris gave me to learn more about global movements and how you could apply those same principles in your context. I teach it in six weeks on Zoom, and I'd love to move our relationship from someone who read my book to a friend! If you're interested email me at: Jim@WhyNotHere.mov

From one disciple maker to another,

Jim

APPENDIX A

topical bible stories

Here is a list of great Bible stories to learn and share that I like to use which relate well to things people are struggling with.

Stories of Hope

Mark 2:1–12 (Healing)

Mark 4:36–41 (Stress)

Luke 15:11–32 (Relationships)

Matthew 14:22–33 (Faith)

Luke 17:11–19 (Gratitude)

Luke 19:1–10 (Hope)

Luke 7:36–50 (Forgiveness)

APPENDIX B

across the table journal sample

prepare

Spend a few moments quietly preparing your heart and mind for the Scripture reading.

When you are ready, choose someone to begin your time together with a short opening prayer.

read Psalm 37:1-9

Read the text carefully and slowly.

Take turns reading out loud, across the table.

meditate

Consider the words of the Scripture. What do they mean to you?

Don't miss the quiet reflection happening across the table from you. There is power and beauty in this time together.

pray

Quietly talk with God, responding to the Scripture and how it spoke to you. These words are between you and God.

contemplate

Pause in silence to consider the Scripture and let God's message to you resonate.

Across the Table journals available to order at: churchleaders.com/discipleship

APPENDIX B: ACROSS THE TABLE JOURNAL SAMPLE

TUESDAY | WEEK ONE

share & connect

Take a moment to share an area where God is meeting you today. Listen to your partner across the table as they share theirs. What is something you've heard in this exchange?

Say a short prayer of gratitude for this time together.

Across the Table journals available to order at: churchleaders.com/discipleship

APPENDIX C

discovery bible study method

LOOK BACK	1. What are you thankful for from this past week? 2. What is a stress or struggle from this past week? *For this question break into partners to share and pray for each other. Write down each other's requests to pray throughout the week.* 3. Can we help with anything shared and does anyone know of a need in the community that we could meet? *Also, follow up with any answers from this question from last week.* 4. What was last week's story? How did your "I will" go? How did it go with sharing it with someone? *This is problem solving accountability. No hint of shame allowed. If the person struggled, ask, "Is it still something you think it would be good for you to do? How can we help you do it this next week?"*
LOOK UP	5. Read this week's story twice. (unless read once up front) 6. Have each person retell it in their own words. *To save time you can break in groups of 2-3 for this part. Have the people listening answer, "Did they leave out or add anything?"* 7. What does this story teach us about God and people? 8. What does it teach us about the life God wants us to live?
LOOK FORWARD	9. How can you practically apply this story to your life this week? "I will..." *Remember to keep it measurable, specific, doable and to write it down.* 10. Who could you share this passage with this week? "I will tell..." *Share a specific name. If you don't have one for this story then share someone you could share another story with.*

APPENDIX C: DISCOVERY BIBLE STUDY METHOD

Stories of Hope: (Jesus)

Luke 17:11–18

Matthew 14:22–33

Mark 4:35–41

Luke 7:36–50

Mark 2:1–12

Luke 19:1–10

Luke 15:11–32

Luke 23:32–42

Luke 24:36–49

Acts 2:37–47

The First Seven Commands

Repent & Believe (Acts 2:38, Luke 19:1–10)

Be Baptized (Acts 2:38,41, Acts 8:26–40)

Pray (Acts 2:42, Matthew 6:9–13)

Love (Acts 2:45, Luke 10:25–37)

Lord's Supper (Acts 2:46, 1 Cor 11:17–34)

Give (Acts 2:44–45, Mark 12:41–44)

Make Disciples (Acts 2:47, Matt 28:16–20)

Creation to the Cross

1. Genesis 1:1–2:3

2. Genesis 2:4–24

3. Genesis 3:1–13

4. Genesis 3:14–24

5. Genesis 6:5–7:24

6. Genesis 8:1–9:17

7. Genesis 12:1–8

8. Genesis 22:1–19

9. Exodus 12:1–28

10. Exodus 20:1–21

11. Leviticus 4:1–35

12. Isaiah 53

13. Luke 1:26–38, 2:1–20

14. Matthew 3:1–17, John 1:29–34

15. Matthew 4:1–11

16. Luke 5:17–26

17. John 3:1–21

18. John 4:1–26, 39–42

APPENDIX C: DISCOVERY BIBLE STUDY METHOD

19. Luke 5:17–26

20. Mark 4:35–41

21. Mark 5:1–20

22. John 11:1–44

23. Matthew 26:17–30

24. John 18:1–19:16

25. Luke 23:32–56

26. Luke 24:1–35

27. Luke 24:36–53

Permission to copy this form for your ministerial use.

APPENDIX D

baptism passages

These are the passages I like to read through with a person who has come to a place where they want to surrender their life to Christ. Let them discover God's next step of obedience for them.

Matthew 3:13–17

Acts 8:26–40

Romans 6:3–5

Acts 2:37–41

Acts 16:11–15, 25–34

1 Corinthians 1:13–17

APPENDIX E

prayer retreat template

Mindset Shift: It was never about "21 days." This journey lasts the rest of your life.

Preparation

- Pick a time where you can carve out around one to three hours.

- Pick a place where you can get away from all distractions (cellphones, social media, kids, spouse, etc.). If weather permits, being out in nature is perfect.

- Bring your copy of this book, a Bible, and pen.

Centering

Take the first few minutes to get your mind off all the things you need to do today to create margin to hear from God today.

> **Read Psalm 23:1-3**
>
> Start writing out a long list of things God has done for you. Think general like creation and salvation, and think specific, like things you've seen him do in your life this week.

Read Psalm 23:4, 5

Write out the stresses and struggles in your life now. One at a time release them to God so your mind is focused to hear from him.

Read Psalm 23:5, 6

Thank him in advance for what He's going to say to you today. Ask for focus to hear and courage to obey.

Introduction

Read the passages mentioned in the Introduction and Days 1-3 just to get your mind focused on the topic of disciple making.

Habit #1: Praying for Someone to Disciple

Write down the things you learned in Days 4-7. How are you going to apply them to your life rhythms going forward?

What is my prayer plan going to be? (The more specific the better.)

Habit #2: Engaging with Potential Disciples

Write down the things you learned in Days 8-11. How are you going to apply them to your life rhythms going forward? Here are some good specific questions to answer:

Who is there already in my life that I need to reach out to? (Who are a few people on my FRANCE sheet I will be reaching out to first?)

Where in my life do I intentionally go to be around lost people?

What are two or three stories that would be good for me to learn for share? (See Appendix A.)

Habit #3: Meeting With My Disciple

Write down the things you learned in Days 12-17. How are you going to apply them to your life rhythms going forward. Here are some good specific questions to answer:

If discovery, obedience, and accountability are key when I'm discipling someone, how can I have those in place in my own life now?

Look over several of the disciple-making tools in the back of the book to decide what you'll use.

Habit #4: Multiplication

Write down the things you learned in Days 18-21. How are you going to apply them to your life rhythms going forward? Here are some good specific questions to answer:

If my end goal is not just to make disciples but make other disciple makers, how will that impact what I do going forward?

Who in my life could I invite to be in a disciple-making community with? Now that I've gone through this book, who should I pass it on to?

Imagination Prayer

Read Ephesians 3:20. Take some time to ask our God who is able to do immeasurably more than all you could ask *or imagine* what you would have Him do through you as you pursue the life of a disciple maker. Write out your specific requests, and use them for how you pray for yourself going forward.

Permission to copy this form for your ministerial use.

ABOUT THE AUTHOR AND ACKNOWLEDGMENTS

Jim Britts has served in Southern California the past twenty-one years as a youth pastor, church planter and currently likes the title of disciple-making movement catalyst. He has a huge passion for equipping and empowering Jesus followers to be disciple makers where they live, work, and play. He's an avid runner, screenwriter, and committed Sacramento Kings fan. Jim has been married to Rachel for twenty-one years. They adopted their first two kids (Jadon and Jordyn) through the foster care system and then immediately had a surprise pregnancy with their third child, Josie.

Acknowledgements

I'm insanely thankful to my incredibly supportive and gifted wife, Rachel. We joke that I write the content but she's the one who makes it enjoyable to read. This disciple-making journey we are on never would have happened without you.

So grateful for Chris Galanos, Suzie Judd, Brent Hofen and the rest of the E-life Disciple Making Coaching community. You inspire me that when it comes to movements here, it's not an *if* but a *when*.

Finally, so thankful for our local team. Trace, Frank, Ion, Burts, Broyles and a ton of others believing in a movement here in North County, San Diego.

21 DAYS TO
Becoming a Disciple Maker